CONTAINER
GARDENING

FOR ALL SEASONS

ANNE SWITHINBANK'S
CONTAINER
GARDENING
FOR ALL SEASONS

photographs by Paul Bricknell

BBC BOOKS

Published by BBC Books,
an imprint of BBC Worldwide Publishing.
BBC Worldwide Limited, Woodlands,
80 Wood Lane, London W12 0TT.

First published 1997
© Anne Swithinbank 1997
The moral right of the author has been asserted

ISBN 0 563 37197 8

Photographs by Paul Bricknell

Illustrations by Jane Cradock-Watson

Designed by Isobel Gillan
Set in Caslon, Copperplate and Garamond

Printed in Great Britain by Cambus Litho Limited, East Kilbride
Bound in Great Britain by Hunter & Foulis Limited, Edinburgh
Colour separations by Radstock Reproductions Limited, Midsomer Norton
Cover printed by Belmont Press, Northampton

Acknowledgements

To write this book it was necessary to design, plant, care for and photograph 50 planted containers. I could not have done all this without considerable help from others. The first task was to source the containers, and a big thanks must go to Kennedy's Garden Centres and most specifically to John Phillips and his team at the Hailsham branch. They kindly allowed me to choose and borrow a wide range of terracotta containers, baskets and a trug. The attractive green 'verdigris'-finished pots and troughs were donated by Tudor Ceramics, Fairhaven Nurseries, Elberton Road, Elberton, Bristol BS12 3AB.

Most of the plants used were bought from a wide range of garden centres and some were used from my own stock of good, container-worthy specimens. Thanks must go to Van Meuwen, PO Box 2, Spalding, Lincolnshire PE12 6NJ, from whom I cadged a few young plants sent by mail order, including Tyrolean carnations.

We grew the containers in our own garden, which meant a lot of watering, feeding and dead-heading. My husband John Swithinbank is in charge of garden projects and it was he who kept the plants growing, a dedicated task through a particularly dry summer. He also warded off small children, curious foxes and marauding crows.

Summer holidays are a worry to most gardeners, but a potential nightmare to those who garden containers. A computerized irrigation system is the ultimate answer, but ours was Michaela Freed, who came in twice a day to look after the plants during our absences.

There was a general air of nervous tension over the household when photography days loomed. Anxious glances were cast at the weather (we could never have moved all the containers under cover at once) and at unopened but promising buds. I must thank Paul Bricknell and his assistant Victoria Gibbs, who were unfailingly cheerful, did not complain at the state of our garage which had to be converted into a photographic studio, or the weather which was occasionally foul. I am also grateful to Jane Coney, design manager at BBC Books, who took a personal interest and came along to make sure that the containers had their good side to the camera.

The last stage of the book was the writing and editing. For their help and encouragement I would like to thank Nicky Copeland and her team, especially project editor Emma Tait. She is intending to buy a flat with a balcony and window ledges, so I am hoping that she will be the book's first convert to container gardening for all seasons.

Contents

——— ◆ ———

Introduction

◆

It is not difficult to understand the appeal of container gardening. For those with no soil beds at all, it means that collections of plants can be enjoyed in window boxes, on balconies and even in tiny courtyards. For those depressed with the state of the rest of their garden, containers can effect a quick facelift. Spend a couple of pleasant hours planting a

smart, terracotta pot and window box, sweep the patio and mow the top part of the lawn for a sudden transformation. In one afternoon a mess can be turned into smart planting around the house with a 'wilderness' in the distance. This book consists of 50 planting ideas which I have designed, planted and cared for. Some have proved particularly enduring and are still being enjoyed in the garden long after their photography was completed.

The first challenge of this book was to decide exactly how the 50 containers should be allocated between the four seasons. The idea of planting for autumn, winter and spring is now firmly entrenched in gardeners' minds. All the same, providing a riot of summer colour is something that pots, boxes and baskets can do so well, especially in otherwise leafy, low-maintenance gardens. So in the end I allocated half of the containers to the summer seasons and the rest of them to the autumn, winter and spring seasons. As with any garden design, it is always the darker months which need the reinforced outlines of good planting design, whereas summer colour is comparatively easy to achieve.

It was so interesting to experiment with plantings using structural evergreens, but also with stems for winter interest. Even now, while writing this introduction, I can feel more ideas coming on. Imagine the bright orange stems of *Salix alba vitellina* 'Britzensis' interplanted with herbaceous plants and clematis for summer. This sort of permanent container planting is particularly useful for balcony gardeners who will not want to change all their plants twice a year.

The methods by which I designed the containers varied. If you know your plants, it is possible to sit at home and sketch an idea for a pot or window box. Planting themes based on a particularly lovely specimen plant, certain colours or an attribute such as shade or drought tolerance come quite easily to mind. The problem with being so specific is that disappointment inevitably follows when tracking down the plants proves difficult and time-consuming.

A useful method is to analyse what is required of a container arrangement, thinking hard about the light it will receive, its shape and general theme, before setting off for the garden centre. Choose a pot or window box and lug it around in the trolley while selecting plants. Or sketch an existing pot, with its dimensions and colour scribbled down. Choose one or more inspiring plants and base the rest on these.

When following my designs, it might not be possible to find all the ingredients in one shopping trip. Be prepared to substitute (which will add individual touches) and to use detective work to track plants down. Serious container gardeners will want to acquire a stock of useful plants and my advice is to buy subjects like hardy perennial evergreens and plant them in the garden (or their own pots if there are no soil beds). They can be lifted and amalgamated into groups with other plants when required. This applies to bergenia (elephant's ears), *Ajuga reptans* (bugle) and *Ophiopogon planiscapus* 'Nigrescens', all of which multiply in a satisfactory way.

Some of my plants, including varieties of shrubby *Euonymus japonicus* and *E. fortunei*, as well as dwarf conifers and winter heathers, have been moved from the garden to containers and back again many times. I would advise saving every small plant of ivy, potting each up and growing them on individually in 10–12cm (4–5in) pots. Mature, long-stemmed ivies lend an air of instant maturity to arrangements. This cultivating of stock plants makes the whole prospect of container gardening more affordable.

While authors writing about trees and shrubs planted permanently into the garden might feel obliged to give dimensions, I have not always done this. The rules are different when plants are containerized, as root growth is restricted, which in turn restricts eventual height. When plants are moved from garden to container or back again, they can be root-pruned to help them grow lots of new fibrous roots and control their size.

There are different ways of tackling container gardening. Pots can be filled with ephemeral plants designed to last only a season. Colourful masses of petunias or marigolds for summer or pansies for winter can be thrown on to the compost heap when they have faded. At the other end of the scale a permanently planted specimen shrub or tree may spend its whole life in a pot or trough and should be looked after well in order to grow and thrive over the years. Both these types of planting are relatively easy to devise, so are not included. To my mind it is putting mixtures of plants together successfully which sets the biggest challenge.

The uses of planted containers are many and varied. Some houses are plain or ugly, but can be transformed by the dual efforts of climbers and container plants. Window boxes, hanging baskets and hay baskets fixed to walls can be filled with leaf and flower to give year-round effect. I use containers in groups to liven up expanses of gravel car-parking areas, to accentuate bends in paths and even to brighten up borders. Planted containers are mobile and can be shifted about the garden to inject colour where it is most needed. Raise them up on bricks to allow for drainage and lift their blooms above other vegetation. This has worked well in one of my borders where the ground-cover rose 'Flower Carpet' pours out of a terracotta pot among groups of sweetcorn, French beans and annual flowers. Pots of structural plants like cordyline (cabbage palm) and agave (century plant) look superb standing among the low plantings of helianthemum (sun rose) on beds mulched with gravel or shingle.

Arrangements of plants in containers do need attention if they are to succeed. View them like miniature gardens and they will thrive and evolve. In common with other garden plants they need water and food, which must be supplied. They also may need to be trimmed and clipped back in order to retain some shape. Where long-lasting specimen shrubs are grown alongside transitory elements like pansies and ivies, they should be given precedence. A light pruning now and again will hold back the swamping stems of ivy and prevent lengthening pansy stems from flopping over neat foliage. Ivies which have been left in a container for several years will need to be lifted, root-pruned and returned if they are not to take over entirely.

Try not to give up on summer containers like hanging baskets. If plants such as lobelia fail, plant some fresh trailing pelargoniums or verbenas into the top, be assiduous with watering, feed regularly and the display will continue until the first frosts.

I have had a lot of fun in the making of this book, both in devising and planting the containers and watching them grow – often out of all recognition. I wish that they could have been photographed twice each, because they changed and evolved as their season of interest wore on. The summer plantings were tight and controlled at the beginning of the season, but spilled over towards the end. Autumn plantings like a mix of *Sedum* 'Autumn Joy' (ice plant) and *Aster amellus* (Italian starwort) looked great in flower but shone during winter too, when their dead flower heads were rimed with frost. Both autumn and winter plantings which held winter-flowering pansies and bulbs burgeoned forth towards late spring as tulips and wallflowers opened their blooms. Even spring plantings designed for instant effect doubled their size, and lasted well, as the fresh leaves of ivies and pretty flowers of *Vinca minor* (lesser periwinkle) unfurled.

Care and Attention

◆

Unlike plants growing in the open soil of beds and borders, those restricted to containers have to rely on somebody to care for them. This commitment need not be onerous and for busy people the routine of watering, feeding and dead-heading their plants can be slotted in at the beginning or end of their working day. If anything, it provides a valuable excuse to slow down for half an hour.

Starting Up

The first consideration is really the choice of container. Terracotta is popular, being both reasonably priced and widely available in many exciting shapes and styles. There are also plenty of glazed clay pots around, decorated with attractive colours which can match or blend with the plants and their surroundings. Containers finished with matt paint are attractive too and can either be bought ready-painted or custom-designed at home.

The main considerations when choosing containers are to make sure that pots and troughs are frost-proof and have one or more drainage holes in the base. Then think about their dimensions and colours.

Where a site is windy and pots of tall plants have been known to roll over, opt for wood. Half-barrels are often more stable, especially when water has soaked into them and, should they be blown over, at least there is no danger of cracking.

Stone containers are heavy and tend to be stable, but are also expensive. Nevertheless a well-chosen urn adds important structure to a garden and will be worth the investment if it helps tie in the landscape and plantings. Simulated and reconstituted stone are cheaper and can still look very convincing, especially when partly covered by plants. Even plain concrete containers can look good in the right settings, especially when weathered and colonized by moss and algae.

Plastic pots usually look cheap and nasty, but can withstand breakage by weather or accident. They also have the huge advantage of being light to carry, which is important to frail gardeners who have trouble lugging heavy clay and wooden containers around. Some do look convincingly like the terracotta or wood they are trying to imitate and I have actually surprised myself by using several for schemes in this book and actually liking them. Smothering the sides with trailing growth creates an effective camouflage.

Compost

There are numerous proprietary composts suitable for container planting, divided into two main types. Loam-based composts have good-quality topsoil as their main ingredient. This will have been sieved to get rid of large lumps, rubbish and stones before being sterilized to ensure that it is reasonably free of pests, diseases and weed seeds. Before it makes a good compost, it has had to be mixed with other ingredients. The most popular recipes are those developed by the John Innes Institute and involve the addition of some peat, sharp sand, a quantity of lime to balance the pH to neutral and fertilizer. Soilless composts contain no loam and might be based instead on peat, coir fibre, finely shredded and composed bark or other waste products.

My preferred compost is a mixture of equal quantities of John Innes No. 2 potting compost and a soilless compost. This is not based on scientific theory but more on a gardener's instinct. A loam-based compost is ideal for containers, especially those planted for autumn, winter and spring. There is more stability, and loam has a natural fertility and mineral content not present in the likes of peat and most waste materials. However, a predominantly loam-based compost seems to benefit from the added texture of

springier, more fibrous, soilless compost. I have used this mixture as the basis for the container plantings in this book. A few proprietary brands come close to this, which saves having to buy two bags and mix them together.

Another ingredient to keep in the shed is horticultural sharp sand or grit. This, when added to a compost, aids the passage of water through it. Using about three parts of ordinary compost to one of grit, a mixture suitable for alpine and succulent plants will be achieved. This is of special merit during winter when it is crucial that these plants are never waterlogged.

Other key additions can include moisture-retaining granules. These swell up in the compost and retain water for the plants. Many gardeners like to use them, especially for hanging baskets which are renowned for drying out rapidly. Follow the packet instructions carefully to avoid adding

too many, as this can be counterproductive. Slow-release fertilizer can also be added to the compost before planting. This is an especially good move for busy gardeners who know that they may not have time to administer regular liquid feeds throughout the summer season. Essential plant foods in slow-release fertilizers become available when temperatures rise sufficiently to encourage plant growth, so these can also be added to winter plantings without encouraging weak growth at the wrong time of the year.

How to Plant

Keeping good drainage firmly in mind, the first task is to find some crocks for the base of the pot or trough. These, when placed over the holes, will prevent them from becoming blocked and will help excess water escape. Ideally the whole base should be covered by crocks to a depth of 2.5cm (1in) or more. Traditionally crocks are pieces of broken clay pot. New gardeners are not likely to have a good supply of these, but can use small stones, expanded clay pebbles (which can be bought in bags), or broken-up polystyrene. Make sure that drainage holes are covered in such a way that water can trickle out.

Next, ensure that the plants are moist in their existing pots. If necessary, dunk the whole pot in a bucket of water until bubbles stop escaping. Congested roots should also be carefully teased out so that they can grow more easily into fresh compost. Even if a few roots become broken in the process, this is still well worth doing. Then pot up. The planting method is straightforward. Put compost into the container, firming gently as it goes in, until the depth is right for the plant with the largest rootball. Position this plant at the correct height, making sure that its best side is towards the front. At this stage it is possible to correct a plant which leans badly by tilting its rootball slightly.

Add a little more compost around the largest plants until it reaches the correct depth for smaller ones and spend some time positioning them until they look just right. Fill in around all the plants until the compost level is within 2.5cm (1in) or so of the top of the container, to allow for watering. The old compost surfaces should all be at the top, just buried by a shallow layer of compost.

While the container is still comparatively light, lift it into its final position. Those destined to stand on garden soil or a flat surface should be raised up slightly to allow water to run away. Use bricks, tiles or special terracotta pot feet. When the container is in place, water the plants thoroughly, using a watering can fitted with a rose (sprinkler). This settles the new compost around the plants without making holes in it. Continue to use a watering can and rose until the plants start to establish themselves.

Hanging Baskets

Hanging baskets need a more specialized approach to planting, and to an extent this is dealt with under each individual container. As a general guideline, and for the process to be as enjoyable as it should be, I recommend gathering everything together first (including a cup or glass of something and the radio). If moisture retention is of paramount importance, opt for a solid plastic basket with a watering reservoir. Solid baskets are less prone to evaporation and extra water stored in the reservoir will help the plants survive searingly hot weather when everybody is out.

HOW TO PLANT A TUB OR TROUGH

1 Cover the base with crocks to a depth of 2.5cm (1in) or more.

2 Dunk any dry plants in a bucket of water until bubbles stop escaping.

3 Tease out congested roots.

4 Build up the compost. Add each plant at the correct depth.

5 Fill around all the plants until the compost level is within 2.5cm (1in) or so of the top.

6 Position the container on feet to raise it. Water using a watering can fitted with a rose.

HOW TO PLANT A HANGING BASKET

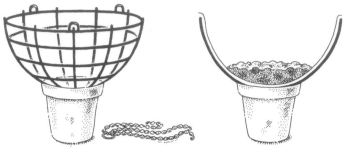

1 Remove the chain and balance the base on a flowerpot for stability.

2 Fit the liner into place and put soil in the base up to the point where the first plants are to be fed into the sides.

3 Force or cut a hole in the liner. Push through the roots of small plants from the outside.

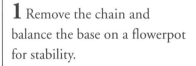

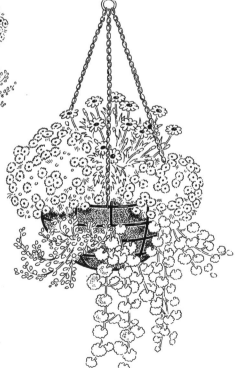

4 If plants have large rootballs wrap their shoots in a square of polythene to make a narrow, protective tube. Then feed this through the liner from the inside out.

5 Build up the compost as plants are added, leaving enough space to arrange plants in the top.

6 Fill around all the roots with compost. Reinforce the moss or moss substitute around the rim of the basket.

The disadvantage of solid sides is that no plants can be inserted here to create the full effect of all-round planting. However, strong, trailing plants like ivy-leaved pelargoniums, trailing fuchsias, *Bidens ferulifolia* and Surfinia petunias will quickly cascade over the edges.

To plant plastic-coated wire baskets, make sure that the chain is removed or on the outside and balance the base on a flowerpot for stability before starting. Fit the liner into place according to its type. Some solid fibre liners need watering before they will relax into the shape of the basket; other more flexible types have slits radiating from the centre, so that when these overlap each other neatly, the liner sinks into a tidy bowl-shape. I still like the texture and flexibility of sphagnum moss and its imitations, cannily made from recycled

materials. The rule with these is not to stint, but use plenty of material to make a good, solid lining. Many gardeners like to place a circle of polythene or a saucer in the base of their lined container, to help retain moisture.

Place soil in the base, up to the point where the first plants are to be fed into the sides. It is best to choose small-rooted plants like trailing lobelia, marigolds, alyssum and the unusual *Gypsophila muralis* 'Garden Bride', which will probably have to be raised from seed, but makes a froth of tiny, pink flowers. Pots of ivy, ajuga (bugle) and *Glechoma hederacea* 'Variegata' (variegated ground ivy or grannilocks) can be divided by cutting through the overground runners binding them together and pulling young plants apart.

The roots of small plants can be pushed through the liner from the outside to sit on the compost. This is simply a question of forcing a hole in the moss or moss substitute, but other liners will have to be cut with scissors or a knife. Where plants with larger roots need to be used, wrap their shoots in a square of polythene to make a narrow, protective tube. Then feed this through the liner from the inside out. When it is safely through, unwrap the shoots and bush them out against the sides. Build up the compost as plants are added, leaving space to arrange plants at the top. Bear in mind that there is little point in planting the sides of the basket that will face the wall or fence. Lastly, fill around all the roots with compost. A final but important touch is to reinforce the moss or moss substitute around the rim of a basket after planting. It is worth having a small bag of this to hand (the manufactured substitutes will keep far better than the real thing). If a purchased flexible liner fails to reach the top of the basket, this moss can be used to plug the gap.

Maintenance

At first, careful watering is all that a newly planted container will require. As far as regularity is concerned, it depends on how much root growth the plants have made, the time of year, whether the container is in the open or in a rain shadow, and if it is in sun or shade. The only way to know when to water is by routinely checking the compost. Containers will even dry out when least expected, during autumn, winter and spring. Summer containers invariably need watering once or even twice a day when established. Never be fooled into thinking that a fall of rain will have soaked the roots, as this is often not the case.

Summer containers full of hungry bedding plants can rarely have too much feed. Even if a slow-release fertilizer has been added to the compost (and these can be added after planting), liquid feeding is still beneficial. Depending on the vigour of the plants used, feeding can take place from once a fortnight or once a week to every day. For those with many containers, it is worth investing in a watering lance with renewable cartridges of fertilizer which release the right dose of plant food into the water. If you are mixing your own, dilute the feed in a small amount of water first by swirling it in the base of the can before filling up. There are many well-balanced liquid fertilizers with added trace elements (small quantities of essential minerals) on the market and most are excellent. If plants seem to need more shoots and leaves, give them a couple of doses of high-nitrogen fertilizer. If they need to produce more blooms or fruit, use a high-potash feed.

Avoid feeding plants when they are wilting for lack of water. It is good practice to give them a soak first, then apply the feed another day when the compost is just moist. In my opinion it is not necessary to apply liquid feed to containers planted during autumn: wait until the weather begins to warm up in spring. There should be enough fertilizer in the compost to give them a boost during the first few weeks of warm, autumnal weather. Any fertilizer applied during winter and early spring is only going to sit around in the compost when there is little or no growth taking place.

Other maintenance consists of keeping plants in good shape by regularly dead-heading fading flowers and removing dead leaves. Pruning back plants which threaten to swamp others can sometimes be prudent, as can trimming up those whose exuberant growths throws the shape of an arrangement out of an otherwise pleasant balance. Simply find the place where a cut is needed, then trim just above a leaf or bud.

Should plants fail or die during the season of interest, take them out and replace them with new ones. It is worth keeping some spare plants in single pots for just that purpose. Many gardeners have returned from holiday to find their container plants clinging to life. A good soak, followed by a liquid feed should precede a thorough evaluation several days later. Dead-heading, trimming and replacement of dying plants should certainly see the container thriving for several more weeks.

Pests and Diseases

The 50 arrangements in this book were remarkably untroubled by pests and diseases. Slugs and snails crept up to have a go at marigolds during the summer and container gardeners need to be on their guard against them. A smearing of petroleum jelly around the pot about half-way up is a good deterrent. Otherwise apply slug control around the base and in the top of the container. Those who use metaldehyde-based slug pellets should note that very few are needed for an efficient control. Clear up dead bodies before birds and other slug predators get to them. Aphids may attack young shoots, but these are usually cleared up by natural garden predators. If colonies are seriously threatening a plant's health, spray with a pirimicarb-based insecticide which will not harm most of the beneficial insects.

Vine weevil larvae are often responsible for plants, notably fuchsias and primroses, collapsing. Investigation will show that their roots have been eaten away by small, beige, C-shaped grubs with dark heads. If there has been a bad attack the preceding year, anticipate more problems and use a biological control. A solution containing a type of nematode (microscopic worm-like creature) which attack and eat vine weevils can be applied to the compost of established plants when temperatures are warm. These nematodes can be ordered through garden centres, or you can buy by mail order from advertisements in gardening magazines.

Overwintering

When tender perennials have finished their stint for the summer, they must be removed before the frosts if they are to be kept for another year. To maintain a range of plants, a frost-free greenhouse, conservatory or porch will be needed. Lift plants like fuchsias, pelargoniums and argyranthemum (marguerite), pot them separately and trim back by about a half before bringing inside. Insulate the greenhouse with bubble plastic, but make provision for opening vents to let air circulate during winter. Pick off dead leaves on plants to reduce the risk of botrytis (grey mould). In late winter, as growth resumes, prune the plants back harder to encourage the best regeneration of shoots. With standards, trim back their heads.

Where there is no greenhouse, it is still worth trying to save plants. Fuchsias can be defoliated and laid down in a trench with a good 23cm (9in) of soil piled on top of them. Mark the spot and lift in spring – at least some will be alive. Pack pelargoniums or fuchsias into a box with polystyrene chippings around the base of the stems for insulation. Keep in a shed and cover with insulating fleece during freezing spells. Water the roots lightly after they have been dry for a while.

Larger specimens like cordylines (cabbage trees) and other tender evergreens likely to be damaged by cold winds can be moved into a greenhouse or, failing this, into a sheltered position. Wrap with garden fleece during the worst weather.

CONTAINERS FOR SPRING

◆

MOST CONTAINERS DESIGNED TO REACH their peak during spring will have been planted up during autumn. This is a natural change-around time when summer bedding plants begin to fade and die, leaving empty containers crying out for a selection of fresh plants.

An autumn planting means time for plants to put down roots while the soil is still warm and moist. On a simple level, masses of polyanthus, pansies or wallflowers will give a lovely display, perhaps with the surprise of bulbs planted beneath them. More sophisticated arrangements can include shrubs and herbaceous perennials, some of which, like Symphytum 'Goldsmith' (variegated comfrey), can be lifted from the garden.

The onset of spring often inspires impulse buying, and in the following pages there are ideas for spring plantings offering instant colour. The likes of pompon bellis (daisy), flamboyant ranunculus and pretty trailing periwinkle give up to three months of pleasure before summer.

Spring Green

◆

Gentle, subtle freshness is the secret behind this pretty arrangement, with flower colour restricted to cream, yellow and dark violet. Plant up in autumn or spring and stand in either a bright position or light shade. Keep out of full sun during summer.

Skimmia × confusa 'Kew Green' provides the main evergreen feature for this container. Deep green leaves are joined, all winter, by heads of tight, pale green flower buds which wait, fist-like, until spring before bursting into large, fragrant clusters of small, creamy-white flowers. Most skimmias are either one sex or the other and this male variety will never set fruit, but could pollinate a nearby female. In spring the lime green of the new shoots is fresh and stimulating. Growing skimmias in pots is a good ploy if plants in the open ground have suffered yellowy-white leaves. This can be caused by wind damage, sun scorch or poor, dry soil.

Set the skimmia to the back of the pot, since it is designed to be viewed mainly from the front. In the foreground, to one side, position a large clump of Vinca minor 'Atropurpurea' (lesser periwinkle) which

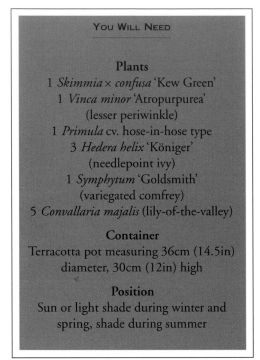

YOU WILL NEED

Plants
1 *Skimmia × confusa* 'Kew Green'
1 *Vinca minor* 'Atropurpurea'
(lesser periwinkle)
1 *Primula* cv. hose-in-hose type
3 *Hedera helix* 'Königer'
(needlepoint ivy)
1 *Symphytum* 'Goldsmith'
(variegated comfrey)
5 *Convallaria majalis* (lily-of-the-valley)

Container
Terracotta pot measuring 36cm (14.5in)
diameter, 30cm (12in) high

Position
Sun or light shade during winter and
spring, shade during summer

has lovely, dark flowers of a deep, plummy purple. In spring the container will be wreathed with stems of both deep green and brilliant lime-green leaves, as well as with flowers. To the other side place an unusual primula like this pale yellow hose-in-hose type. This plant is so named because one flower appears to sit inside the other.

All that remains is to take three pots of plain green *Hedera helix* 'Königer' (needlepoint ivy), divide each pot into two and set them around the edge to fill any gaps. Finally make a space in the middle ground to accommodate a potful or root of *Symphytum* 'Goldsmith' (variegated comfrey), which will brighten the arrangement with gold-margined, sage-green leaves. Palest pinkish-blue flowers appear in spring. As a finishing touch, plant a few roots of lily-of-the-valley along the front of the container, wherever a small gap can be found.

Place in a shady position for summer and, with some tidying, this can brighten another winter and spring. Trim back in autumn and plant out the comfrey, replacing it with winter-flowering pansies.

Skimmia × confusa
'Kew Green'

Convallaria majalis
(lily-of-the-valley)

Symphytum 'Goldsmith'
(variegated comfrey)

Primula cv.
hose-in-hose
type

Vinca minor
'Atropurpurea'
(lesser periwinkle)

Hedera helix 'Königer'
(needlepoint ivy)

Tulipa 'Gordon Cooper'

Myosotis
(forget-me-not)

Hedera helix cv.
(cream-variegated ivy)

Ivy Swag and Tulip Pot

◆

The simplest ideas are often the best, and containers planted with spring bulbs which rise up and flower through a sea of pansies, wallflowers, polyanthus or forget-me-nots are beautiful and effective. Plant up during autumn so that roots can establish themselves for the best spring blooms. A position of good light is beneficial for this container.

There are many combinations of bulbs and other spring flowers to try, but one of my favourites is tulips with an underplanting of forget-me-nots. As there will be little autumn and winter colour, add swags of ivy to provide structure.

Three compact and mature cream-variegated ivies with plenty of long stems are needed to create an instant effect. Place some compost in the base of the pot, so that the ivies will be at the correct height, then space them evenly around the edge. Take the nine young forget-me-not plants and position them at the correct height so that two plants sit around the edges between each ivy, with three for the centre. Before filling in with compost, add the tulip bulbs 15cm (6in) deep by digging small holes for them between the myosotis. For this container the Darwin hybrid *Tulipa* 'Gordon Cooper' was chosen for its single, salmon-pink flowers which change to scarlet as they mature, on stems 60cm (2ft) high.

After filling in around all the roots with potting compost and watering, tie the ivies into swags. Divide the stems of each plant into two, and bring the right-hand half of one together with the left-hand half of its neighbour so that they make a swag over the edge of the pot. Using garden twine, tie the stems together. Repeat this with the other ivies, making sure that the depths of the three swags match all round the pot.

As spring turns to summer the tulips and forget-me-nots will fade and should be removed. If the tulip leaves are still green, transfer the bulbs into good garden soil; after the leaves have yellowed they will be worth lifting to store, dry and plant out next autumn. Forget-me-nots will seed into the garden, providing a self-replenishing ground cover of blue spring flowers, so it may be worth planting them out too, to make sure that their seed ripens and falls.

I would leave the ivy swags, add shade-tolerant summer bedding plants – impatiens (busy Lizzie), mimulus (monkey flower), begonia or fuchsia. Plant up with fresh spring-flowering plants the following autumn.

YOU WILL NEED

Plants
3 *Hedera helix* cv. (cream-variegated ivy)
9 *Myosotis* (forget-me-not)
8 *Tulipa* 'Gordon Cooper'

Container
Painted terracotta pot measuring
37cm (15in) diameter, 34cm (13in) high

Position
Good light in winter and spring, but shade
during summer

Ranunculus Trough

◆

This short window box relies upon the strong shapes of double ranunculus flowers for its impact. Plant up in spring and place in a well-lit position for the best results.

These amazing, double ranunculus have been bred from *Ranunculus asiaticus*, an eastern Mediterranean species. Although it is possible to grow ranunculus from their claw-like, fleshy roots, more reliable results are obtainable from ready-grown plants. For one thing the roots are not widely available in autumn, which is when you would need to plant. Second, coaxing plants into full bloom simultaneously for a spring planting would take luck and skill. In spring there are plenty of good-quality, potted ranunculus in the garden centres, bursting with promising buds. So plant up in spring for some instant colour.

YOU WILL NEED

Plants
2 *Vinca minor* (lesser periwinkle)
3 *Ranunculus* cv. (white ranunculus)
2 *Ranunculus* cv. (red ranunculus)
2 *Hedera helix* cv. (plain green-leaved ivy)
8 *Muscari armeniacum* (grape hyacinth)

Container
Short, decorated terracotta trough measuring 35cm (14in) long, 27cm (11in) high

Position
Well lit

Place some compost in the base of the container and position one good clump of *Vinca minor* (lesser periwinkle) at each end.

Position the ranunculus at the correct height towards the back and middle of the trough. There is a variety of colours available, but here three taller, white-flowered plants were used for the back, with two shorter, red-flowered varieties for the middle. To furnish the front, position two plain green-leaved ivies there.

Finally dobble individual *Muscari armeniacum* (grape hyacinth) throughout the trough wherever there is room. Then fill in with potting compost. These muscari can be bought by the potful and carefully separated or, with planning, can be potted up as bulbs in the autumn and left outside to grow naturally. They can even be lifted carefully direct from the ground despite their deep roots.

Although the plants have been disturbed and moved around, they settle in quickly and will give pleasure and colour for the next six weeks. After flowering and when they have died down, plant the ranunculus roots into the garden 5cm (2in) deep in well-drained soil and full sun. Alternatively store them dry in pots with a little soil covering to prevent undue shrivelling throughout summer and pot them up properly in autumn. Plant the *Muscari armeniacum* 5cm (2in) deep into the garden. They are good garden plants because, unlike the more common *M. neglectum*, they do not become invasive. Plant out or pot up the vinca and ivies.

Ranunculus cv.
(white ranunculus)

Vinca minor
(lesser periwinkle)

Ranunculus cv.
(red ranunculus)

Hedera helix cv.
(plain green-leaved ivy)

*Muscari
armeniacum*
(grape hyacinth)

Euonymus fortunei
'Silver Queen'

Arabis alpina ssp.
caucasica 'Snowcap'

Viola tricolor
(heartsease pansy)

Arabis and Pansies

◆

This shallow, basket-weave pot is the ideal container for a pretty and festive spring arrangement. It is crucial that the container and its plants are in scale with one another. A pack of arabis proved the initial inspiration and the remaining plants were carefully lifted from the garden. Although this container could be planted up in autumn (all the ingredients are evergreen), it was, to be honest, an example of instant gratification.

Had I planted this up in autumn, I might well have included some small bulbs, bright blue *Scilla siberica* (Siberian squill) perhaps, or one of the tiny, early-flowering species crocus. I avoid the bright yellow varieties, since the sparrows seem to like tearing their blooms.

With petals like confetti, pretty, pure white *Arabis alpina* ssp. *caucasica* 'Snowcap' needed companions of a delicate but festive nature. The cream-edged leaves of *Euonymus fortunei* 'Silver Queen' seemed just right. Good plants should not be hard to find in garden centres and will prove, as mine has, to be useful stock for containers. Trim back long shoots to retain a compact shape.

Viola tricolor (heartsease pansy) seeds itself with abandon. I allow it to grow where it will, weeding it

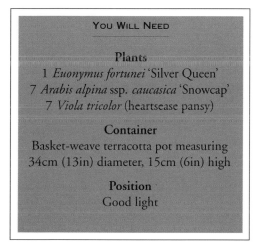

YOU WILL NEED

Plants
1 *Euonymus fortunei* 'Silver Queen'
7 *Arabis alpina* ssp. *caucasica* 'Snowcap'
7 *Viola tricolor* (heartsease pansy)

Container
Basket-weave terracotta pot measuring
34cm (13in) diameter, 15cm (6in) high

Position
Good light

out if space is needed for other plants. Small plants start to flower in spring and continue through to late summer, when young seedlings begin to show and persist throughout winter for next year's flowers. These pretty little plants with their typical pansy faces seemed ideal companions for the arabis, so seven were carefully lifted for the spring pot. Again they and other dainty, seed-raised violas are easy to find at your local garden centre. Once they have been introduced to the garden, they should be self-renewing.

Begin by placing some compost in the base and positioning the euonymus in the middle of the pot. Then simply add a little more compost around the sides to raise it to the right height for the arabis and violas, which can be alternated all the way around the edge before the final filling-in with compost.

When the arabis have finished flowering, gently dismantle the container. Find a well-drained site alongside a path, or in a rock or dry garden where the arabis can spread themselves into 25cm (10in)-wide clumps. Plant them and then trim off their dead flowers. *Viola tricolor* can be planted out too and will seed themselves all over the place. Plant the euonymus as a shrub in the border or keep it to one side for future use as a container specimen.

Basket of Bellis and Grape Hyacinths

◆

This subdued but pretty spring basket was photographed in a cold mid-spring. By late spring it had matured to reveal a fine mass of lemon-yellow wallflowers in the centre with pretty, blue periwinkles, the pompons of double pink bellis and strands of variegated ivy cascading down the sides. Plant the basket in autumn, or even in spring, and enjoy the gentle spring colours.

Many wallflowers come in orange and mahogany shades which, though bright and cheerful, are not spring-like, so opt for a lemon-yellow- or white-flowered variety for a soft effect. Having lined the basket, place some potting compost inside and position the wallflowers in a central group. The three large bellis can then be placed evenly around them towards the edges.

Some bellis have small, button-like flowers, while others bear huge, double powder-puff-like blooms. These are hardly subtle, but pale pink or white are good spring colours.

Since this basket was to hang in a rather windy position, it seemed more sensible to use tough trailing ivies to cascade over the edges rather than plant in the sides. Either search out long-stemmed

---

YOU WILL NEED

Plants
3 *Erysimum cheiri* cv. (lemon-yellow wallflower)
3 *Bellis perennis* cv. (double pink daisy)
2 *Hedera helix* 'Goldchild' (variegated ivy)
1 *Vinca minor* (lesser periwinkle)
6 *Muscari latifolium* (grape hyacinth)

Container
Plastic-coated wire hanging basket measuring 35cm (14in) diameter

Position
Good light during winter, but shade for summer

---

ivies or use plants salvaged from past containers. The ivy used here is not one of the hardiest, but came through the winter well.

Few plants can rival ivies for their trailing foliage during autumn, winter and spring. This periwinkle is a contender, but really competes well only in spring when dull winter foliage is joined by new, lime-green leaves and pretty blue flowers. Here, it has been used to fill a gap at the back.

Muscari latifolium (grape hyacinth) can be inserted as bulbs into gaps between the plants during an autumn planting, before the final addition of compost. For a spring planting buy a potful, separate individual plants from each other and drop them into dibber holes; alternatively fork up a clump carefully from the garden.

By late spring take one of two actions. You can either remove the bellis and wallflowers, replacing them with shade-tolerant summer bedding plants like impatiens, mimulus, fuchias, moving the basket to a shady position. The alternative is to dismantle the container, putting the vinca and muscari into the garden, potting up the ivies and discarding the rest.

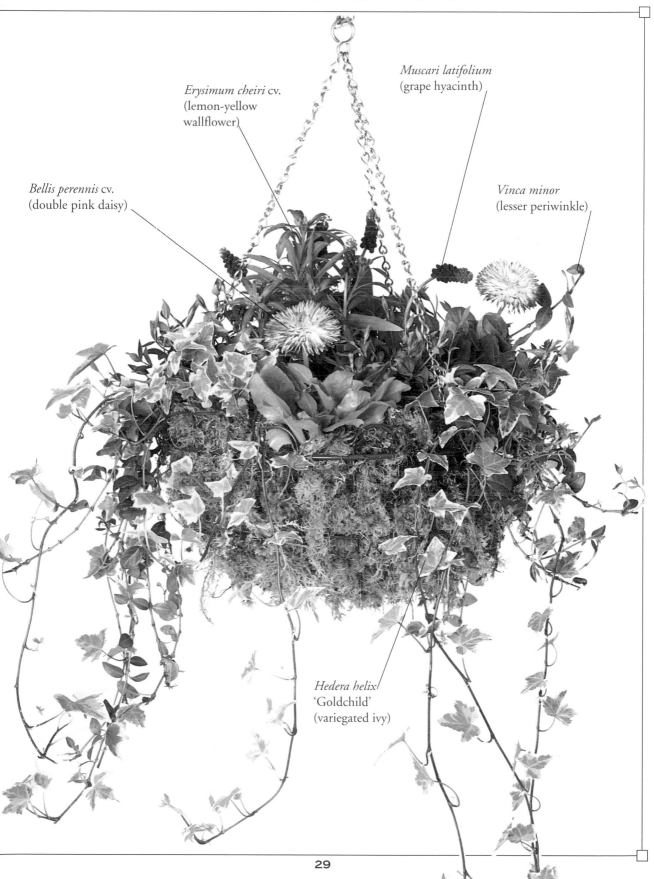

Erysimum cheiri cv.
(lemon-yellow
wallflower)

Muscari latifolium
(grape hyacinth)

Bellis perennis cv.
(double pink daisy)

Vinca minor
(lesser periwinkle)

Hedera helix
'Goldchild'
(variegated ivy)

Tulipa 'Toronto'

Eyrsimum cheiri cv.
(yellow and red
wallflowers)

Viola × *wittrockiana* cv.
(red pansy)

Viola × *wittrockiana* cv.
(yellow pansy)

Pedestal of Tulips and Wallflowers

◆

Leaving behind the delicate yellow, white and pink colours of early spring, this pedestal planting is designed to peak in late spring with a riot of warm gold, mahogany, red and orange. Plant up in the autumn so that the wall-flowers in particular can establish some root growth before winter. Stand away from the drip of trees.

Select wallflowers carefully in the autumn, to ensure that those sold bare-rooted are still in good condition. Their roots should not have been dried out, frozen or waterlogged. It is often possible to buy smaller, potted plants, which might be safer. Alternatively home-grown wallflowers are not difficult, but will tie up space during summer. If there is a spare row in a vegetable plot free of club root (to which they are prone), simply sow seed thinly into drills across a seedbed in early summer. When large enough to handle, transplant 15cm (6in) apart and grow on until needed in autumn.

Before planting the container make sure that there is plenty of drainage material such as crocks or broken polystyrene in the bottom. Put in some potting compost, then position the wallflowers in the centre of the planter, making sure the two colours are well mixed. Take three each of red and

---

YOU WILL NEED

Plants
3 *Erysimum cheiri* cv. (yellow wallflower)
3 *Erysimum cheiri* cv. (red wallflower)
3 *Viola × wittrockiana* cv. (red pansy)
3 *Viola × wittrockiana* cv. (yellow pansy)
10 *Tulipa* 'Toronto'

Container
Terracotta pedestal urn measuring
35cm (14in) diameter, 44cm (17.5in) high

Position
Good light

---

yellow winter-flowering pansies and alternate them around the edge. Long-stranded ivies could also be used here to mask an ugly pot.

When the main plants are in place and at the correct height, start planting tulip bulbs so that they will eventually be covered with 15cm (6in) of potting compost. Any medium-height, warm-coloured tulip will suit this arrangement, but *Tulipa* 'Toronto' was chosen. This Greigii hybrid is multi-headed, with two to three rose-vermilion blooms opening at the top of each 30cm (12in) flower stem. However, plans do not always succeed in gardening and my tulips were only single-headed, though they were of the right colour. The effect was still stunning.

Endless variations on a similar theme can be tried, using one or more layers of bulbs to push through a planting of forget-me-nots, *Erysimum × allionii* (Siberian wallflower), primroses or bellis. The absence of evergreens with bulky roots means the tulip bulbs can be distributed evenly around the container.

When the final flowers fade on pansies and wallflowers, the planting can be dismantled and the tulips moved to the garden.

Alpine Window Box

◆

For those who love alpine plants yet have no garden, this window box is an ideal solution. Although it is predominantly planted with spring-flowering alpines, there will be plenty here to offer seed heads and flowers in summer and foliage for winter. This idea will also suit those who would like an interesting window box without the twice-yearly effort of replacing annual and tender perennial bedding plants. For these alpines are hardy, perennial and, with the right care and attention, should last many years. Plant up in spring and place on a sunny window ledge.

To create a strong seasonal impact, two plants of *Pulsatilla vulgaris* (pasque flower) were used. To create structure and symmetry the *Rhodanthemum hosmariense* (formerly *Leucanthemum hosmariense*) were used in a pair too. For greater year-round appeal choosing just one each of these would free spaces to allow the introduction of more evergreen alpine plants.

Good drainage is of paramount importance when growing alpines, so make sure that the trough has adequate drainage holes. These should be covered with a good layer of crocks, pebbles or broken polystyrene. Add an extra quantity of grit or sharp sand to the usual potting mix – say, about three parts of potting compost to one of grit. This will help excess water pass easily through the compost and out of the base.

To plant, place some potting compost over the drainage layer and position one rhodanthemum at each end. This worthy plant, from the Atlas Mountains in Morocco, bears white daisies above silvery, evergreen, fern-like foliage and carries on blooming throughout summer and into autumn. A good, large clump of *Phlox subulata* 'Amazing Grace' (moss phlox) in the centre can flop elegantly over the edge. Expect a long succession of palest pink flowers into early summer, each with a deep pink centre. It is evergreen and will not die back in winter. In the gaps at the back, position two *Pulsatilla vulgaris* (pasque flower). Even though they die down in winter, they are good value, not only for their delicate foliage and colourful flowers, but also because of their enduring, fluffy seed heads. These will make good clumps in the container and seed can be used to raise yet more plants for a well-drained position in the garden.

YOU WILL NEED

Plants
2 *Rhodanthemum hosmariense*
1 *Phlox subulata* 'Amazing Grace' (moss phlox)
2 *Pulsatilla vulgaris* (pasque flower)
1 *Sedum spathulifolium* 'Cape Blanco' (stonecrop)
1 *Anthemis marschalliana*
6 *Scilla siberica* (Siberian squill)

Container
Terracotta trough measuring 60cm (2ft) long,
17cm (7in) wide, 16cm (6.5in) high

Position
Sunny

Into the remaining gaps at the front insert one *Sedum spathulifolium* 'Cape Blanco' (stonecrop) for its silvery-grey, evergreen foliage. If any brittle stems fall off during planting, pop them into a small pot of gritty compost to make more plants. Finally add *Anthemis marschalliana*, originally from the Caucasus, which bears small, yellow flower heads over silvery, filigree leaves.

For a touch of blue, buy or grow a pot of *Scilla siberica* (Siberian squill), divide into single bulbs and dot them throughout the container. These will provide bright, early colour, producing their flowers on plants 10–15cm (4–6in) high. Fill in around all the roots with the gritty potting mixture, then top off with gravel. This looks good, saves water splashing on delicate leaves and holds in moisture. Maintenance consists of watering when necessary and applying a light dressing of general-purpose fertilizer the following and succeeding springs. Trim back wayward plants after they have flowered and add replacements if any should die or outgrow the container.

Rhodanthemum hosmariense

Sedum spathulifolium 'Cape Blanco' (stonecrop)

Pulsatilla vulgaris (pasque flower)

Anthemis marschalliana

Phlox subulata 'Amazing Grace' (moss phlox)

Scilla siberica (Siberian squill)

Narcissus tazetta ssp. *lacticolor*

Erysimum 'Bowles' Yellow' (perennial wallflower)

Bellis perennis cv. (double white daisy)

Hedera helix 'White Knight' (variegated ivy)

Yellow-and-white Basket Planter

◆

Baskets make cheap containers for the garden and are useful for new gardeners who may need more clay pots than they can afford to buy. The wicker-work will not last as long as clay, but gradually weathers over several years before beginning to fall apart. This cheerful spring combination of white and yellow flowers can be planted in autumn for good root establishment, or on impulse in spring, and will enjoy full sun.

Line the basket with black polythene before planting. Old compost bags opened out and reversed are useful for this. I usually cut out a large square, push it inside, make holes in the base and trim to leave 5–8cm (2–3in) which can be folded back and tucked in. The focal specimen here is *Erysimum* 'Bowles' Yellow' (perennial wallflower).

One large wallflower or three smaller ones can be placed towards the middle and back of the container. Three double white bellis can then be slotted at even distances around the edge. Arrange two large, long-stemmed ivies so that their dangling stems of leaves can weave through the basket handles and flow over the edges.

Having positioned all these at the correct heights, add some narcissus bulbs before finally filling in around the plants with potting compost. Choose petite narcissi like *Narcissus tazetta* ssp. *lacticolor* (formerly *N. canaliculatus*), a native of Mediterranean regions, which grows from 15 to 50cm (6 to 20in) depending on soil conditions. Each stem bears three to four scented flowers with yellow cups surrounded by slightly backswept, white petals. The bulbs should be covered by about 8cm (3in) of compost after all the gaps have been filled in around the plant roots.

If planting takes place in spring, it is possible to buy pots of *N. tazetta* in bud. Carefully separate the bulbs and dig narrow planting holes for them between the other plants, so that they look as natural as possible.

When spring is over and the flowers begin to fade, it is best to dismantle the container. Plant the *Erysimum* 'Bowles' Yellow' out in the garden, pruning the tops back by half after they have settled in to encourage compact, new growth. It is also possible to take cuttings of new shoots, to raise plants for future containers. Make a group of the narcissus in the garden and pot up the ivies.

YOU WILL NEED

Plants
3 *Erysimum* 'Bowles' Yellow'
(perennial wallflower)
3 *Bellis perennis* cv. (double white daisy)
2 *Hedera helix* 'White Knight' (variegated ivy)
9 *Narcissus tazetta* ssp. *lacticolor*

Container
Wicker basket measuring 30cm (12in) diameter,
30cm (12in) high

Position
Good light

Yellow-and-bronze Bowl

◆

This combination of yellow with bronze-purple is symbolic of the kind of spring ground cover you might find between shrubs in a border. A wide terracotta bowl is deep enough for the largest rootballs, yet remains in scale with the rest of the arrangement. Plant in autumn or spring and stand in sun or semi-shade.

Three main plants form the backbone of this bowl. *Euphorbia amygdaloïdes* 'Purpurea' (wood spurge) bears reddish-bronze leaves which change to bright lime green towards the tops where flowers begin to form. As with all spurges, take care when handling as the sap can irritate the skin. Position this euphorbia first, towards the middle and back of the container, before placing the dense, evergreen *Euonymus japonicus* 'Golden Maiden' next to it.

To complete the threesome, add an interesting *Helleborus × sternii* Blackthorn Group (hellebore). This strain has the advantage of being short as well as blessed with fascinating colours. The combination of crimson stems with silvery foliage and pink-flushed flowers is most distinctive.

To the back of the taller plants will be a gap, which can be plugged with a *Bergenia cordifolia* (elephant's ears). These useful, evergreen, ground-cover plants with distinctive leaves, are easy to grow from seed. A seedling with particularly purple-bronze leaves was used here.

Flower colour is provided by simple, yellow *Primula vulgaris* (primrose). Space three plants out around the front, interspersed with a couple of clumps of *Hedera helix* cv. (cream-variegated ivy) and groups of *Ajuga reptans* 'Braunherz' (bugle).

Important colour is also provided by cheerful *Narcissus* 'Tête-à-Tête'. If the planting takes place in autumn, make holes with your fingers before filling in with compost and slip bulbs in here and there around the central plants. For a spring planting buy a pot of bulbs, separate them and plant where required.

To fill remaining gaps around the edges, I carefully lifted self-seeded *Viola riviniana* (dog violet) out of the garden and planted them here and there (you can, or course, buy violets from a garden centre). The effect was charming and long-lasting.

YOU WILL NEED

Plants
1 *Euphorbia amygdaloïdes* 'Purpurea' (wood spurge)
1 *Euonymus japonicus* 'Golden Maiden'
1 *Helleborus × sternii* Blackthorn Group (hellebore)
1 *Bergenia cordifolia* seedling (elephant's ears)
3 *Primula vulgaris* (primrose)
2 *Hedera helix* cv. (cream-variegated ivy)
2 *Ajuga reptans* 'Braunherz' (bugle)
5 *Narcissus* 'Tête-à-Tête'
9 *Viola riviniana* (dog violet)

Container
Terracotta bowl measuring 57cm (23in) diameter, 23m (9in) high

Position
Good light in spring (light shade in summer)

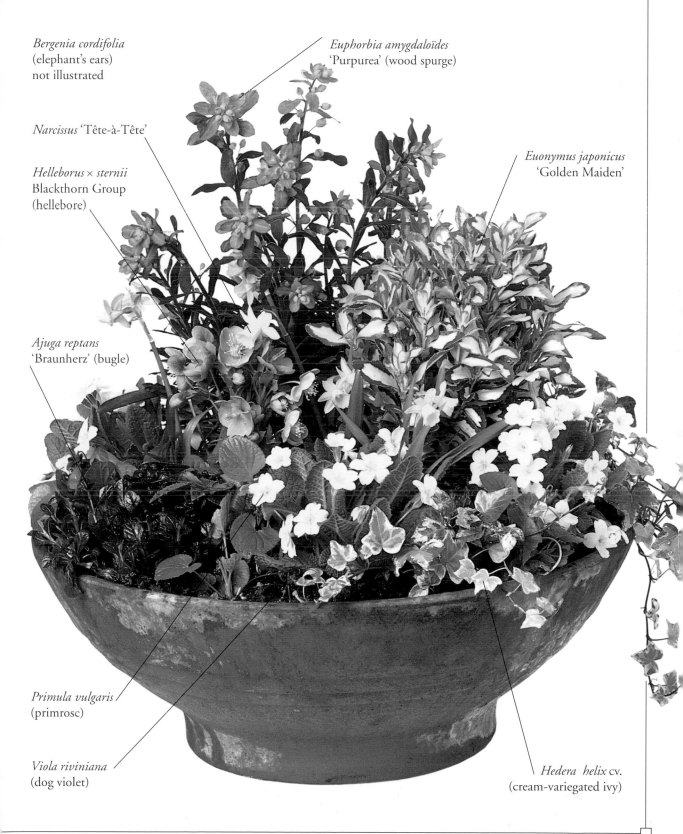

Bergenia cordifolia
(elephant's ears)
not illustrated

Euphorbia amygdaloïdes
'Purpurea' (wood spurge)

Narcissus 'Tête-à-Tête'

Euonymus japonicus
'Golden Maiden'

Helleborus × sternii
Blackthorn Group
(hellebore)

Ajuga reptans
'Braunherz' (bugle)

Primula vulgaris
(primrose)

Viola riviniana
(dog violet)

Hedera helix cv.
(cream-variegated ivy)

CONTAINERS FOR SUMMER

◆

SUMMER CONTAINERS ARE FUN TO put together because of the exciting plants available and the fast rate of growth during spring and summer. The popularity of container gardening over the past decade has certainly been matched by the range of plants available from garden centres.

Whether the planting becomes a showy, floriferous mass or a demure, shade-tolerant arrangement, whether it consists of native herbs or alpines or is an unusual, drought-tolerant composition, there is one common factor. Even if the plants are small to begin with, they will grow out of all recognition when the magic ingredients of water and food are added to warm summer temperatures and long days.

Most summer containers are planted in spring and cannot be put outside until late spring or early summer when the danger of frost has passed. There is also room for impulse summer planting later in the season, to give extra colour to revive a flagging garden or help celebrate a special occasion.

Alpine Strawberry Pot

◆

Terracotta strawberry pots with planting pockets around the sides make ideal containers for alpine plants. For those who cannot install a rock garden, here is an ideal, space-saving way to enjoy these plants. Plant in spring and keep in full sun.

Good drainage is vital, starting with a properly functioning hole in the base, which should be covered by a 5cm (2in) layer of crocks, stones or broken polystyrene. To three parts of the usual loam and soilless compost mix (see page 11), add one part of sharp sand or grit.

Choose one plant for each hole, plus four for the top, opting for evergreen, compact plants which will creep over the pockets. *Armeria maritima* (sea thrift) gradually engulfs the hole with its tufts of narrow leaves and heads of small, pink flowers on long stalks. *Dianthus* 'Inshriach Dazzler' is superb, with dense leaves and flowers on narrow stalks. *Sempervivum* sp. (houseleek) will rise up to flower during summer, but for variation in foliage colour, choose silver-grey *Sedum spathulifolium*

YOU WILL NEED

Plants
1 *Armeria maritima* (sea thrift)
1 *Dianthus* 'Inshriach Dazzler' (not illustrated)
1 *Sempervivum* sp. (houseleek)
1 *Sedum spathulifolium* 'Cape Blanco' (stonecrop)
1 *Geranium dalmaticum* (miniature cranesbill)
1 *Papaver miyabeanum* (alpine poppy)
2 *Lewisia* cv.
1 *Thymus* × *citriodorus* (lemon thyme)
1 *Saxifraga* 'Silver Cushion'
1 *Anthemis marschalliana*.
1 *Frankenia thymifolia* (not illustrated)

Container
Terracotta strawberry pot measuring 19cm (7½in) diameter, 47cm (19in) high

Position
Full sun

'Cape Blanco' (stonecrop). *Geranium dalmaticum* is a miniature cranesbill with pretty, shell-pink flowers, and *Papaver miyabeanum* (alpine poppy) from Japan is short-lived, but sends up a reliable succession of pale yellow flowers. Strawberry pots are just right for lewisias, because these fussy plants can be planted in them at a sideways angle, enabling rain to run off during winter.

Place some compost in the base, up to the bottom of the first pockets. Position the first layer of plants, then fill in with compost to the second layer, and so on to the top. Then place the remaining three or four plants around the edge. Leave a sufficient gap in the top for a final layer of shingle or stone chippings.

Add any extra compost needed to the side pockets and finish these off with shingle. Water in, sprinkling water into the pockets as well as over the top.

Care consists of keeping the compost moist and applying just a couple of doses of well-balanced liquid feed during summer. In spring trim back the foliage of plants like thyme.

Geranium dalmaticum
(miniature cranesbill)

Sempervivum sp.
(houseleek)

Thymus × *citriodorus*
(lemon thyme)

*Anthemis
marschalliana*

Saxifraga 'Silver
Cushion'

...*isia* cv.

Sedum spathulifolium
'Cape Blanco'
(stonecrop)

Armeria maritima
(sea thrift)

Papaver miyabeanum
(alpine poppy)

Lewisia cv.

Lilium 'Reinesse'

Lavandula stoechas leucantha (white French lavender)

Dianthus cv. (bedding dianthus)

Antirrhinum 'Lampion Pink' (trailing snapdragon)

Hedera helix cv. (cream-variegated ivy)

Impatiens 'Cherry Blush' (busy Lizzie)

Lily Pot

◆

Most summer containers are planted up in late spring so that they can grow and knit well together. Sometimes, though, the need arises for some instant colour later in the season. A strategic container may fade as a special occasion approaches, or the garden may simply need brightening up in late summer. By this time the choice of bedding plants in the garden centres has dwindled, so look instead at summer-flowering bulbs and small shrubs as the main components of your display. This pot was assembled only a few days before the photograph was taken and is an example of instant container gardening. Stand the pot in sun or light shade.

A good container gardener who has collected plenty of plants together will probably only have to purchase just two or three new plants to make this arrangement or something similar. The feature plant here is white-flowered *Lilium* 'Reinesse'. This and others like it are easy to find in bud at garden centres from mid-summer onwards. Alternatively the need for fresh colour could be anticipated in spring and a few bulbs potted then.

YOU WILL NEED

Plants
1 pot of *Lilium* 'Reinesse' (3 bulbs)
1 *Lavandula stoechas leucantha*
(white French lavender)
1 *Hedera helix* cv. (cream-variegated ivy)
1 *Dianthus* cv. (bedding dianthus)
1 *Impatiens* 'Cherry Blush' (busy Lizzie)
1 *Antirrhinum* 'Lampion Pink'
(trailing snapdragon)

Container
Glazed terracotta pot measuring
35cm (14in) diameter, 30cm (12in) high

Position
Sun or light shade

Lilies rising up from lavender is one of my favourite combinations, and *Lavandula stoechas leucantha* (white French lavender) makes a lovely companion. Distinctive in having white bracts protruding from the top of the flower spike, this has a different perfume from English lavender. A good pot of cream-variegated ivy saved from previous winter containers will balance the white lavender.

Garden centres do still have some bedding plants in mid-summer, but the range tends to be smaller and the plants larger. Inject some strong colour by choosing a bedding dianthus.

It also pays to keep a few spare summer bedding plants, potting them on into 10cm (4in) pots. From my stock of a dozen or so plants were chosen this pale pink, dark-eyed *Impatiens* 'Cherry Blush' (busy Lizzie) and *Antirrhinum* 'Lampion Pink' (trailing snapdragon) to fill in remaining gaps to the front.

When the lily bulbs have finished flowering, remove the dead flowers and let the stems die back naturally. In early autumn the bulbs can be planted out into the garden. At the end of the season the lavender can be made use of in borders and the ivy in another container.

Fennel Hanging Basket

◆

Hanging baskets can be rather predictable if similar plants are used repeatedly. To create a more individual note, try picking one striking plant as an anchor, in this case the pink-and-white candy-striped petunias. Then trawl the garden centre to find plants which can blend with their splendid gaudiness. Plant up in late spring.

Purple fennel is an unusual choice for a hanging basket, yet looks superb, making a fine mass of feathery purple foliage. Judicious pruning will help keep it within bounds. Purple sage seems a good choice too. Both act as a great foil to the huge purple/pink-and-white petunia blooms.

YOU WILL NEED

Plants
6 *Lobelia* 'Fountain Lilac'
6 *Alyssum* 'Easter Bonnet Violet' (not illustrated)
1 *Foeniculum vulgare* 'Purpureum' (purple fennel)
1 *Salvia officinalis* 'Purpurascens' (purple sage)
3 *Petunia* cv. (pink-and-white candy-striped petunias such as P. Ultra Series)
1 *Pelargonium* 'Matisse'
(double trailing geranium)
1 *Verbena* 'Loveliness' (lavender trailing verbena)
2 *Hedera helix* 'White Knight' (variegated ivy)
1 *Brachycome* 'Tinkerbell' (Swan River daisy)

Container
Ironwork hanging basket measuring
37cm (15in) diameter

Position
Sun

The first task, when planting, is to furnish the sides of the basket with trailing *Lobelia* 'Fountain Lilac' and *Alyssum* 'Easter Bonnet Violet'. Position the liner, then some compost in the base. Part the moss, or make holes in the liner with scissors or a knife, in order to position four of each sort around the sides facing front.

Build up the compost in the centre and place the fennel centrally, with the sage just in front. Then snuggle the three striped petunias in around them. Add to the trailing effect by setting in place a cerise, trailing *Pelargonium* 'Matisse' (double trailing geranium) and lavender-blue-flowered *Verbena* 'Loveliness' (trailing verbena) to the sides and red-stemmed *Hedera helix* 'White Knight' (variegated ivy) to the centre.

There will be odd gaps here and there, which can be filled by using up the remaining two each of lobelia and alyssum. Finally find space for a lovely, blue *Brachycome* 'Tinkerbell' (Swan River daisy).

In the early stages of development the arrangement was neater than the picture shows, with more alyssum in bloom. The proof of any good basket lies in its keeping qualities. By the end of summer it was still attractive, with only the alyssum disappearing under a mass of growth. A mid-season manicure is a good idea when young; dead-heading and pruning back of over-enthusiastic, uneven growth works wonders.

At the end of the season plant out the fennel (but let it seed only if you want it all over the garden) , pot up the ivy and pelargonium.

Foeniculum vulgare
'Purpureum'
(purple fennel)

Verbena 'Loveliness'
(lavender trailing
verbena)

Petunia cv.
(pink-and-white candy-
striped petunia)

Lobelia
'Fountain Lilac'

Hedera helix 'White
Knight' (variegated ivy)

Salvia officinalis
'Purpurascens'
(purple sage)

Pelargonium 'Matisse'
(double trailing
geranium)

Brachycome 'Tinkerbell'
(Swan River daisy)

Versailles Tub

◆

Large containers can support many plants, achieving a wonderful riot of colour throughout summer. Although they are potentially costly to fill, here is a great excuse for a potted version of Victorian sub-tropical bedding. When planting a Versailles tub (or, more correctly, a *caisse*), first decide where the front will be. Organize the plants so that they cascade from tall at the back to small and trailing at the front. Plant this arrangement in late spring and stand in the sun.

Position the main plants for height first, starting with *Anisodontea capensis*. This pretty, half-hardy, South African perennial of the mallow family bears many tiny, saucer-shaped, pink flowers. To one side of it, in the far corner, plant a good-sized specimen of *Tibouchina urvilleana* (Brazilian spider flower) which will wait until late summer and early autumn before opening its large, stunning, purple-blue flowers with dark, spider-like stamens. To fill the back add the hardy, evergreen, silvery-grey-leaved shrub *Brachyglottis* 'Drysdale'. To the front of these, *Fuchsia* 'Thalia'

will make a fine, upright bush of dark foliage, with orange flowers.

A *Fuchsia* cv. with a good bushy shape can fill one side, with *Rosa* Regensberg (dwarf floribunda rose), to the front. Position the two *Petunia* 'Surfinia Purple' to trail over the sides, then go about filling in any spaces. As gap fillers, *Hyssopus officinalis* (hyssop) and *Nicotiana alata* 'Fragrant Cloud' add perfume. Hyssop provides aromatic foliage, while the tobacco plant opens its lovely, sweetly perfumed, creamy-white flowers in the evening.

After a couple of weeks begin adding a well-balanced liquid fertilizer to the water every fortnight. At the end of the season remove the plants. *Anisodontea capensis, Tibouchina urvilleana* and the fuchsias can be potted up to overwinter in a frost-free greenhouse. In spring, prune the anisodontea and tibouchina by half and the fuchsias quite hard.

Brachyglottis 'Drysdale', the rose and hyssops can be planted out in the garden as they are hardy. Hyssop dies back for the winter and the nicotiana and petunias are best composted.

YOU WILL NEED

Plants

1 *Anisodontea capensis*
1 *Tibouchina urvilleana*
(Brazilian spider flower)
1 *Brachyglottis* 'Drysdale'
1 *Fuchsia* 'Thalia'
1 *Fuchsia* cv. (any bush-shaped variety)
1 *Rosa* Regensberg
(dwarf floribunda rose)
2 *Petunia* 'Surfinia Purple'
3 *Hyssopus officinalis* (hyssop)
3 *Nicotiana alata* 'Fragrant Cloud'
(tobacco plant)

Container

Square, dark green plastic Versailles tub (*caisse*) measuring 51cm (20.5in) square at the top, 47cm (19in) high

Position

Sun

Tibouchina urvilleana
(Brazilian spider flower)

Anisodontea capensis

Nicotiana alata
'Fragrant Cloud'
(tobacco plant)

Fuchsia 'Thalia'

Brachyglottis
'Drysdale'

Hyssopus
officinalis (hyssop)

Fuschia cv. (any
bush-shaped
variety)

Rosa Regensberg
(dwarf floribunda rose)

Petunia
'Surfinia Purple'

Euonymus japonicus
'Microphyllus
Pulchellus'

Tropaeolum
'Peach Melba' (nasturtium)

Scaevola aemula
'Blue Fan'

Fuchsia 'Brutus'

Chimney Pot

◆

Chimney pots are desirable containers, especially to lend height to a composition of several pots and bowls. They can also be difficult to find and expensive to buy. The alternative, of buying a plastic chimney pot, might seem unattractive, but once planted it can look quite smart and on a good day can be mistaken for the real thing. Plant the chimney pot in spring.

Tall, narrow containers are often hard to plant up, because the few plants which can be squeezed in the top have to work hard to produce a good volume of growth in proportion to the length of the pot. Stems are also needed to spill out over the sides.

I have seen trailing *Glechoma hederacea* 'Variegata' (variegated ground ivy) used effectively for the sides, and it takes up very little room in the top. Tradescantias (inch plants) are also useful. These, along with chlorophytums (spider plants), are examples of houseplants well worth propagating for use in summer containers.

For this pot there are four plants which share equal dominance. Begin the planting by steadying the base and making sure that water can escape through the pot. This plastic container has a base, with drainage hole. Place a couple of bricks in the

---

YOU WILL NEED

Plants
1 *Fuchsia* 'Brutus'
1 *Scaevola aemula* 'Blue Fan'
1 *Euonymus japonicus* 'Microphyllus Pulchellus'
3 *Tropaeolum* 'Peach Melba' (nasturtium)

Container
Grey plastic chimney pot measuring 25cm (10in) diameter, 60cm (2ft) high

Position
Sun

---

bottom with some stones on top for stability. Then fill the bottom half as thoroughly as possible with some broken-up polystyrene. Trickle the compost on top. Press down and firm.

Real chimneys have no base, and are trickier to plant. One useful method is simply to find a large pot or hanging basket which will fit snugly and securely in the top. Sit it in place and use this for planting. The alternative is to position the pot where it will not have to be moved until the end of the season. Then use the brick, stone and polystyrene method.

Build up the compost so that plants can be positioned in the top, placing the *Fuchsia* 'Brutus' and *Scaevola aemula* 'Blue Fan' at the front, the bushy *Euonymus japonicus* in the middle to add bulk and the three *Tropaeolum* 'Peach Melba' (nasturtium) plants at the back. 'Peach Melba' is an upright variety which flowers quite late, though the unusual peachy-coloured flowers with darker markings are worth waiting for.

The *Scaevola aemula* 'Blue Fan' is a recent introduction and is loved for its unusual, fan-shaped, blue flowers. This and the fuchsia can be overwintered as plants or cuttings. At the end of the season plant out the euonymus.

Daisy Hay Basket

◆

This subtle planting makes a shimmering mass of pink and white daisies over a sea of silvery foliage. A hay basket can be fiddly to plant initially, but makes an attractive feature against a wall. The back of the planter is sheltered from drying winds and it is therefore less prone to drying out than a hanging basket. Plant up in late spring and display in a sunny position.

Lining a hay basket needs some forethought as the holes in the framework are usually too wide for moss to be used on its own. There are purpose-made liners, but finding one to fit the basket can be tricky. They can be lined with polythene, and empty compost bags used black side out are ideal. Alternatively buy a length of nylon greenhouse shading material or closely woven garden netting and use this as a liner. Push into the basket with some overlapping on the outside, which can be tucked in or trimmed off after planting.

Some hay baskets have a solid basin at the bottom which can cause waterlogging of the compost. If yours is one of these, place a good layer of crocks, stones or broken polystyrene in the base before adding compost. You can introduce plants to the sides by cutting small holes in the liner and feeding them in.

For this container *Glechoma hederacea* 'Varie-gata' (variegated ground ivy) was used for its long skeins of growth. One potful can sometimes be divided into two or three small plants by carefully nipping off the running stems which join the plants together. They will then slot easily into the sides.

Three plants were chosen to space out along the top of the container. *Argyranthemum* 'Petite Pink' is a lovely, compact marguerite ideal for baskets or boxes under windows where tall plants would obscure the view from inside. Two plants of small-leaved *Helichrysum microphyllum* were positioned along the front of the container and the remaining gaps filled by six plants of seed-raised *Brachycome* 'White Splendour' (Swan River daisy).

At the end of the season it is worth digging out, potting and saving the pink argyranthemums. They need cool, bright, frost-free overwintering quarters, but can be used again in successive years. It is possible to save helichrysum and glechoma too. The brachycome can be composted and raised again from seed the following year.

YOU WILL NEED

Plants
1 *Glechoma hederacea* 'Variegata'
(variegated ground ivy)
4 *Argyranthemum* 'Petite Pink' (marguerite)
2 *Helichrysum microphyllum*
6 *Brachycome* 'White Splendour'
(Swan River daisy)

Container
Plastic-coated wire hay basket measuring
67cm (27in) long, 17cm (7in) wide (at widest
point), 17cm (7in) deep (at deepest point)

Position
Sunny

Brachycome
'White Splendour'
(Swan River daisy)

Argyranthemum
'Petite Pink' (marguerite)

Helichrysum
microphyllum

Glechoma hederacea
'Variegata'
(variegated ground ivy)

Phormium 'Bronze Baby'
(New Zealand flax)

Bidens ferulifolia cv.

Antirrhinum 'Lampion
Yellow' (pale yellow
trailing snapdragon)

Fuchsia 'Genii'
(bushy, gold-leaved
fuchsia)

Petunia cv. (red-and-
white petunias)

Phormium Pot

◆

This abundant potful gradually changed from being quite an orderly arrangement in early summer to the blowsy mass of yellow daisies pictured here at the end of the season. Plant up in late spring and stand in a sunny position.

The main character plant at the centre of this exuberance is *Phormium* 'Bronze Baby' (New Zealand flax). It has attractive, dark purple-bronze, sword-like foliage and does not grow as large as the species. All the phormiums make dramatic container plants, whether on their own or mixed with other plants. I find them far tougher and hardier than the various kinds of cordyline (cabbage palm) which, though they often weather a winter, can end up with disfigured leaves, especially in an open position.

Begin by placing the phormium centre-back, then slot a bushy, gold-leaved fuchsia in front, for a striking combination of bronze and yellow. Alternatively use a good-size plant of *Cuphea ignea*, the pretty cigar plant, with its narrow, reddish-orange, tubular flowers. This can usually be found in the houseplant section of a garden centre, but will grow outdoors during summer.

YOU WILL NEED

Plants
1 *Phormium* 'Bronze Baby'
(New Zealand flax)
1 *Fuchsia* 'Genii'
(bushy, gold-leaved fuchsia)
2 *Bidens ferulifolia*.
3 *Petunia* cv. (red-and-white petunias)
Antirrhinum 'Lampion Yellow' (pale
yellow trailing snapdragon)

Container
Glazed terracotta pot measuring
35cm (14in) diameter, 30cm (12in) high

Position
Sun

Place the two innocent-looking, young plants of *Bidens ferulifolia*, a native of South America and Mexico, at the edge on either side of the phormium. As youngsters they already have lengthening stems, but be prepared for a great flourish of growth. These are not good plants for the tidy-minded. Around the sides slot in three large-flowered petunias. I chose a variety with white-centred, warm red flowers so that the three predominant colours are bronze, yellow and red. Finally, tuck a small plant of *Antirrhinum* 'Lampion' (pale yellow trailing snapdragon) in the front to one side.

At the end of the summer carefully remove the plants, pulling away the bidens and petunias. It is possible to root cuttings from and overwinter the bidens, but it is the fuchsia and phormium which are really worth saving. At the end of the season, they can be planted out in the garden.

The phormium can be repotted into the centre of the container as a winter feature. This could be accompanied by yellow and red pansies or bronze *Ajuga reptans* (bugle). A phormium will also enhance border plantings. Once established it proves usefully drought-tolerant.

Summer Trug

◆

Containers of all sorts can be used for planting and there is no reason to feel restricted to pots, troughs and hanging baskets. Look about for novel containers and use practically any vessel through which excess water can escape. Old colanders, Wellington boots, chimney pots and kettles furnished with adequate drainage holes have all been successfully planted. On a larger scale I have seen tyres, empty oil drums and sinks put to use. In the absence of these, garden centres and shops do have alternatives to buy. This trug, for instance, was planted in late spring.

For effective planting, tailor the plant choice to the type and size of container so that they remain in proportion to each other. For a trug a fairly low planting is appropriate, with no need for a tall feature plant. It has to be said that a random mixture of low-growing bedding plants would look fine, but for something more designed, choose a set of dominant plants, like these deep, richly coloured petunias. These are of the Grandiflora type, which have large flowers. The drawback is that, although young plants are compact, stems grow longer and longer as the season progresses. There is of course the new *Petunia milliflora* 'Fantasy' to choose now, which is compact and eminently suited to containers. Its flowers, though, are small and would not have had the same impact.

Having carefully lined the trug with black polythene, with holes made in it for drainage, add some compost and position the three petunias in the middle. Three wide-growing *Felicia amelloïdes* 'Variegata' (kingfisher daisy) can then be added at each end. With a completely different habit and texture, these stiff-stemmed kingfisher daisies will spread nicely and flower reliably all summer. I had two plants of double blue *Lobelia* 'Kathleen Mallard' in the greenhouse, so added these too.

Any remaining spaces can be filled with soft-shaded 'Watercolour' (pansy). For the first few weeks the plants were low and the handle of the

---

YOU WILL NEED

Plants
3 *Petunia* cv. (pink Grandiflora type)
3 *Felicia amelloïdes* 'Variegata' (kingfisher daisy)
2 *Lobelia* 'Kathleen Mallard'
7 *Viola* × *wittrockiana* 'Watercolour' (pansy)

Container
Garden trug measuring 40cm (16in) long,
25cm (10in) wide

Position
Sun

---

trug prominent. As summer progressed all the plants grew up to smother the handle and make a fine show. The trick here is to choose plants which manage not to swamp each other as they grow.

At the end of the summer season only the felicia and lobelia are worth saving. Take cuttings of both plants in mid-summer, so that they can be overwintered in a cool, bright, frost-free place. The old plants can be kept too if there is space. The rest can be consigned to the compost heap. Dry the trug out thoroughly and store in a dry place until it is needed again.

Viola × wittrockiana 'Watercolour' (pansy)

Petunia cv. (pink Grandiflora type)

Felicia amelloïdes 'Variegata' (kingfisher daisy)

Lobelia 'Kathleen Mallard'

Perilla frutescens var.
crispa

Abutilon 'Joan Patricia'

Pelargonium cv. (red
zonal pelargonium)

Coreopsis verticillata
'Zagreb'

Brachycome
'White Splendour'
(Swan River daisy)

Helichrysum petiolare
'Limelight'

Abutilon Pot

◆

Warm colours are the inspiration behind this fine summer arrangement. The pale orange terracotta pot, two-toned from watering and weathering, blends well with the apricot bells of *Abutilon* 'Joan Patricia'. Plant up in late spring and place in full sun.

Having started off with the pot and the abutilon, it took a while to track down another tall plant whose foliage could act as a backdrop to the abutilon stems. *Perilla frutescens* var. *crispa* fitted the bill perfectly, with its dark, almost black, crinkle-edged foliage capable of adding substance while not competing for attention. Perilla is an aromatic plant in the family Labiatae, whose square stems mark them out from most other plants. The leaves can be used in cooking and are popular in other countries (mainly eastern Asia). An annual, it can be raised from seed.

Position the abutilon and perilla together, so that the perilla is right at the back of the container with the abutilon in front. Then add the soft-leaved *Helichrysum petiolare* 'Limelight'. Widely used in containers, this variety has golden leaves and makes a good edging. Two were used at the front and one to cover the bare area at the back.

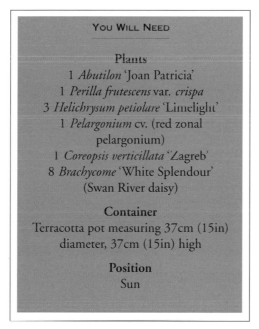

YOU WILL NEED

Plants
1 *Abutilon* 'Joan Patricia'
1 *Perilla frutescens* var. *crispa*
3 *Helichrysum petiolare* 'Limelight'
1 *Pelargonium* cv. (red zonal pelargonium)
1 *Coreopsis verticillata* 'Zagreb'
8 *Brachycome* 'White Splendour' (Swan River daisy)

Container
Terracotta pot measuring 37cm (15in) diameter, 37cm (15in) high

Position
Sun

This will leave a middle space, which can be filled with three groups of plants. To provide a spot of bright red use a red-flowered zonal pelargonium (geranium).

For a burst of yellow, add one good-sized plant of *Coreopsis verticillata* 'Zagreb'. This is a draught-tolerant, herbaceous perennial boasting fine foliage and many flowerheads. A froth of white, daisy flowers can be achieved by finding space for eight small plants of *Brachycome* 'White Splendour' (Swan River daisy). These were seed-raised, because it is more often the purple and blue varieties of Swan River daisy which appear for sale.

At the end of the season pot up the pelargonium and abutilon to overwinter in cool, bright, frost-free quarters. Abutilon remains a good stock plant for future containers. It is possible to overwinter helichrysum too, but cuttings are difficult to root and plants can succumb to a damp atmosphere. The coreopsis can be planted out in the garden, where it will die back for winter, but eventually make a clump which can be lifted in spring and divided to service future containers. The rest of the plants are best consigned to the compost heap.

Sunshine Hanging Basket

◆

Hanging baskets which work well for me are those, like this, which develop beautiful outlines. A tallish plant ususally graces the top with growth cascading down and around the sides, finally trailing away at the base. Plant up in late spring and position in full sun. Despite its fragile appearance, this combination lasted well in a vulnerable position exposed to sun and drying winds.

As with most hanging baskets, work starts with a plastic-coated wire basket balanced on a wide flowerpot. This stops it from wobbling about while you are planting into the sides. Line first with either a good layer of sphagnum moss or a flexible,

ready-made liner. Place some potting compost in the base, then proceed to plant up the sides.

In the search for an alternative small plant to use instead of the ubiquitous trailing lobelia, try *Tagetes* 'Lemon Gem'. This resembles a small-flowered, bushy French marigold, with fern-like leaves. They are particularly successful during the earlier weeks of the basket's life. In addition to five tagetes and five trailing lobelia, add five *Glechoma hederacea* 'Variegata' for their dangling stems of rounded, variegated leaves. Two potfuls will probably yield five individual plants if carefully separated by severing spreading stems and dividing the roots.

Having filled in with more compost, it is time to plant the top. As a specimen plant for the middle, *Argyranthemnum gracile* 'Chelsea Girl' (marguerite or Paris daisy) proves splendid, with plenty of small, white daisies over bluish-green, fern-like foliage. Around this position three *Verbena* 'Booty' (trailing verbena) at equal distances from each other. Fill the gaps with two *Helichrysum petiolare* 'Limelight', a *Fuchsia* 'Display' (trailing fuchsia) and two *Lysimachia* 'Golden Falls'. Any remaining gaps can be plugged with extra tagetes.

At the end of the season lift and pot up the argyranthemum, verbenas and fuchsia. The glechoma and lysimachia might be worth saving, all requiring a cool, bright, frost-free place in which to overwinter. The helichrysum often succumb to winter damp.

YOU WILL NEED

Plants
7 *Tagetes* 'Lemon Gem'
5 *Lobelia* 'Fountain Lilac' (trailing lobelia)
5 *Glechoma hederacea* 'Variegata'
(variegated trailing ground ivy)
1 *Argyranthemum gracile* 'Chelsea Girl'
(marguerite or Paris daisy)
3 *Verbena* 'Booty' (trailing verbena)
1 *Helichrysum petiolare* 'Limelight'
1 *Fuchsia* 'Display' (trailing fuchsia)
2 *Lysimachia* 'Golden Falls'

Container
Plastic-coated wire hanging basket measuring
35cm (14in) diameter

Position
Sun

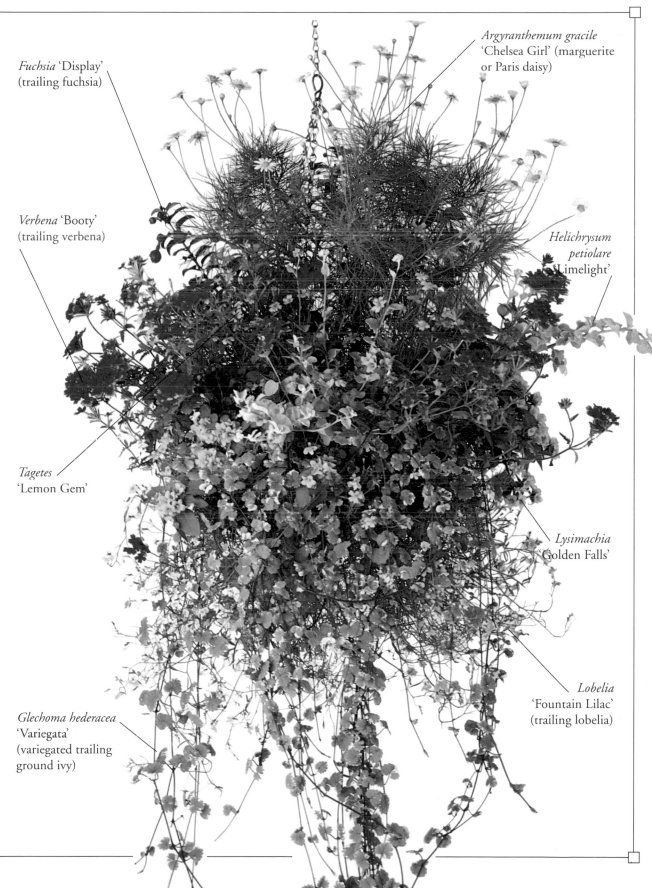

Argyranthemum gracile
'Chelsea Girl' (marguerite
or Paris daisy)

Fuchsia 'Display'
(trailing fuchsia)

Verbena 'Booty'
(trailing verbena)

*Helichrysum
petiolare*
'Limelight'

Tagetes
'Lemon Gem'

Lysimachia
'Golden Falls'

Lobelia
'Fountain Lilac'
(trailing lobelia)

Glechoma hederacea
'Variegata'
(variegated trailing
ground ivy)

Eucomis bicolor
(pineapple bulb)

Eucalyptus gunnii
(cider gum)

Ursinia pulcherrima
'Dwarf Solar Fire'

Portulaca grandiflora cv.
(sun plant)

Pelargonium
'Harlequin Mahogany'
(double-flowered, ivy-
leaved pelargonium)

Exotic Pot

◆

This arrangement is for gardeners who grow tired of seeing combinations of the same old bedding plants in containers. Widen the net and there are all kinds and colours of shrubby, herbaceous and bulbous plants with the only drawback of costing more to buy initially. The results will be unusual, exciting container plantings and a collection of perennials which will last for more than one season. This lively composition should be planted in spring and placed in full sun.

The South African *Eucomis bicolor* (pineapple bulb) is hardy in milder areas. The large bulbs come on to the market in spring and can be planted either singly 5cm (2in) deep in 15cm (6in) clay pots, or three to a 23cm (9in) pot. Grow them initially in a frost-free greenhouse.

Allow the young plants to produce their basal tuft of leaves before placing them in the container. From this tuft they will send up a maroon-speckled stem with buds at the top. These open slowly to a spike of greenish-cream flowers edged with maroon, crowned with a tuft of leafy bracts.

Mixing continents thoroughly, the silvery-grey leaves of Australian *Eucalyptus gunnii* (cider gum)

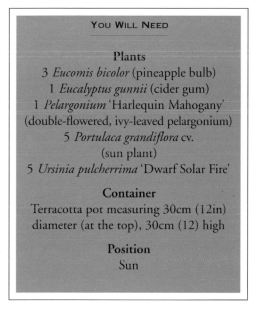

You Will Need

Plants
3 *Eucomis bicolor* (pineapple bulb)
1 *Eucalyptus gunnii* (cider gum)
1 *Pelargonium* 'Harlequin Mahogany'
(double-flowered, ivy-leaved pelargonium)
5 *Portulaca grandiflora* cv.
(sun plant)
5 *Ursinia pulcherrima* 'Dwarf Solar Fire'

Container
Terracotta pot measuring 30cm (12in)
diameter (at the top), 30cm (12) high

Position
Sun

make an ideal backdrop for the eucomis, and together they form the main body of the planting. Position them first, then place the *Pelargonium* 'Harlequin Mahogany' (double-flowered, ivy-leaved pelargonium) to trail over the front. Fill in around this with a double-flowered form of succulent trailing *Portulaca grandiflora* (sun plant), originally from South America.

Finish off by plugging the remaining gaps with South African *Ursinia pulcherrima* 'Dwarf Solar Fire'. I make spring sowings of this pretty hardy annual in trays in the greenhouse. Do not overfeed this arrangement as the plants originate from areas where the soil is quite poor. A general-purpose liquid feed every fortnight should be ample. At the end of the season pot the eucomis and put it in the greenhouse or a frost-free place to die down. Keep dry during winter, but water in spring as growth starts. The eucalyptus can be potted or planted out in the garden; to keep a plant bushy with juvenile foliage, cut the stems almost to the base in spring. The trailing pelargonium can be overwintered in frost-free quarters, but the ursinia and portulaca can go on the compost heap.

Trough of Blue and Silver

◆

This silvery-blue trough can be used as a window box or free-standing. Watching the arrangement evolve throughout summer was a pleasure. A central silvery mound was created by a duo of *Senecio cineraria* and the grass *Festuca glauca*. On either side of this, crisp white-flowered bedding carnations made a backdrop for the small, blue flowers of *Scaevola* and *Lobelia richardsonii*. The interesting, pinkish apricot blooms of diascia added a touch of warmth. By the end of summer it had become a riot of leaves and flowers.

Senecio cineraria (formerly *Cineraria maritima*) is a useful plant for containers, making a solid block of silvery foliage. It can be grown from spring-sown seed, but is also readily available in plant form. It is evergreen during milder winters

and doubles as a winter foliage plant. Cut back old foliage in spring and this sub-shrub will even perform for another summer.

To add a different texture choose the fescue, a tough, hardy grass of diminutive proportions which fits well into arrangements, adding a soft, needle-like effect. Towards late summer it produces feathery, brownish-coloured flowers which will complement the warm apricot blooms of the diascia.

Position the senecio and festuca to form a silver-grey mass of foliage in the centre back. The bedding carnations placed one on either side of these are grown as annuals and make small, bushy plants which have two main flushes of bloom during summer.

Trailing plants used to decorate the front quickly grow out of their initial neat shapes into wayward stems of flower. The scaevola, a relative newcomer to the container-plant scene, has purplish-blue flowers borne all summer. The perennial, blue-and-white-flowered lobelia is more robust than annual lobelia, with tougher stems and a more enduring nature. The two plants used here along the front made a fine mass of resilient growth.

Diascias are useful for containers and filled a small gap in this asymmetrical arrangement. Even here, after a long season of flowering, there are still blooms forming on the stem tips and an

YOU WILL NEED

Plants
1 *Senecio cineraria*
1 *Festuca glauca* (blue fescue)
2 *Dianthus caryophyllus* cv. Knight Series (white bedding carnation)
1 *Scaevola aemula* 'Blue Fan'
2 *Lobelia richardsonii*
1 *Diascia barberae* 'Blackthorn Apricot'

Container
Short terracotta trough measuring 36cm (14.5in) long, 18cm (7in) wide, 18cm (7in) deep

Position
Sun

interesting tracery of old flowering stems. Diascia flowers are double-spurred, apparently to encourage bees which stick their front legs down the spurs to collect nectar, a performance during which they also dust themselves with pollen.

At the end of the season the senecio can continue as an evergreen container plant in mild areas. The festuca can be added to the beds or borders of a garden. Diascias, perennial lobelia and scaevola can all be overwintered in a cool, bright, frost-free place, preferably as young plants raised from summer cuttings. The carnations will have to be composted and are best bought in again for the following year.

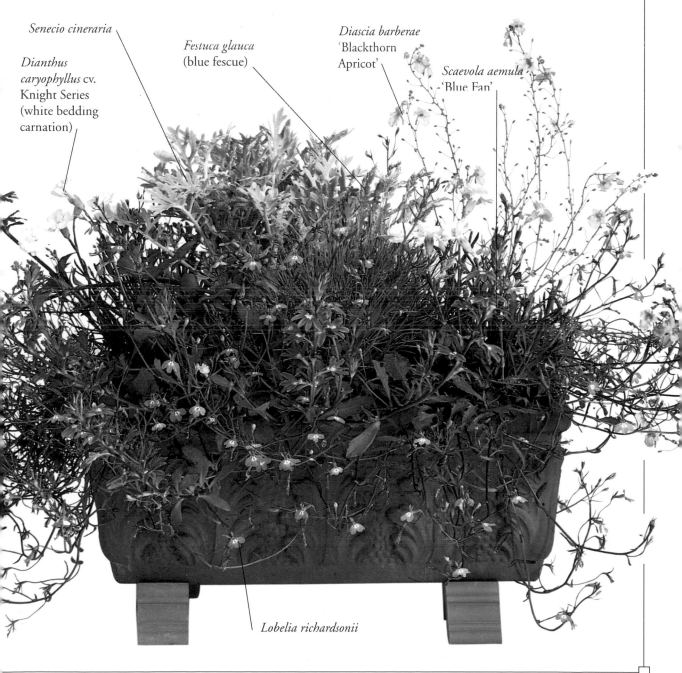

Senecio cineraria

Festuca glauca (blue fescue)

Diascia barberae 'Blackthorn Apricot'

Scaevola aemula 'Blue Fan'

Dianthus caryophyllus cv. Knight Series (white bedding carnation)

Lobelia richardsonii

Petunia (white Grandiflora type)

Argyranthemum foeniculaceum (marguerite or Paris daisy)

Tyrolean carnations

Pelargonium cv. (double lilac-flowered, ivy-leaved pelargonium)

Helichrysum petiolare 'Variegatum'

Fuchsia 'Annabel'

Basket Weave Planter

◆

This was one of a pair of baskets, each planted as a mirror image of the other, which stood like festive sentries on either side of a path all summer. The combination of silver and white with just a few touches of colour proved elegant and took on an interesting, glowing quality at dusk. Plant in late spring and stand in sun.

Baskets are a cheaper and more rustic alternative to terracotta, concrete or stone. They will last for several seasons, gradually fading and weathering with age. For a longer life line them with polythene cut from old compost bags, so that the black side faces outwards. This will also stop compost from falling through the holes. It is vital to make slits in the bottom and to put in a generous layer of stones or polystyrene so that excess water can escape easily.

Canary Island marguerites or Paris daisies are deservedly popular for containers of all kinds and *Argyranthemum foeniculaceum*, along with *A. frutescens*, was one of the first to be widely available. Masses of small, white daisies, produced all summer long, are a feature of both, but *A. foeniculaceum* is also blessed with extra finely cut, ferny, blue-green foliage. Place a good, strong plant

---

YOU WILL NEED

Plants
1 *Argyranthemum foeniculaceum*
(marguerite or Paris daisy)
1 *Fuchsia* 'Annabel'
1 *Pelargonium* cv. (double lilac-flowered,
ivy-leaved pelargonium)
1 *Helichrysum petiolare* 'Variegatum'
3 *Petunia* cv. (white Grandiflora type)

Container
Wicker basket measuring 30cm (12in)
diameter, 30cm (12in) high

Position
Good light

---

to the middle-back of the basket, then position *Fuchsia* 'Annabel' just to the front of it. Lovely pink-tinged, creamy-white flowers contrast well against fresh, light green foliage.

Trailing effect is going to be provided by a double, lilac flowered, ivy-leaved pelargonium on one side and silvery, felt-leaved *Helichrysum petiolare* 'Variegatum' on the other. If a pair of baskets is to match, stand them together and plant simultaneously. When it comes to the trailing plants, place the two ivy-leaved pelargoniums so that their stems reach towards each other. The helichrysums will then both be on the outside.

Fill in gaps with three white, large-flowered petunias. For a touch of bright red, three plants of trailing Tyrolean carnations have also been added, but these are optional. For more punch and less daintiness, the fuchsia could be substituted with a couple more petunias.

At the end of the season, carefully remove and pot the marguerite, pelargonium and fuchsia and place them in a cool, bright, frost-free place to overwinter. A good pruning-back in spring will encourage them to regenerate fresh shoots of leaves and flowers.

Begonia Basket for Shade

◆

Hanging baskets are often needed to cheer up the shadier walls of buildings, but plants for these positions should be carefully selected. Sun-lovers will become drawn in low light and often refuse to flower. Above all shady places need warm colours. Plant up in late spring and hang in shade or semi-shade.

For this basket first select a sizeable specimen of trailing tuberous begonia. Then the other plants can be chosen to tone in with it. Stand a plastic-coated wire basket on a flowerpot for stability and line with sphagnum moss or a suitable flexible liner. Place some compost in the base and start planting the sides.

For the sides, shade-loving mimulus (monkey musk) are ideal for their speckled, warm-coloured flowers. If their rootballs are too large to fit through the wire sides from the outside, wrap the foliage in tubes of polythene and feed them carefully out from the inside, so that their rootballs sit on the compost. Once through, the rather brittle shoots can be carefully unwrapped.

Mimulus come in shades of cream, pink, orange and deep orange, but sadly there were no flowers open on the day of our photography as they tend to open in spurts throughout summer.

Having planted the sides, build up the compost inside so that the begonia will be at the correct height in the middle. Position shrubby *Euonymus fortunei* 'Emerald 'n' Gold' there too, for its warm gold-and-green foliage. Set two *Lysimachia nummularia* 'Aurea' (golden creeping Jenny) and an ivy around the sides and add more mimulus in the gaps.

The plants matured gradually throughout summer, giving interest from day one to a great crescendo of tumbling, orange flowers, warm, speckled blooms and skeins of trailing, golden foliage in autumn.

At the end of the season the begonia can be lifted, potted and dried out to overwinter in a frost-free greenhouse. Start into growth again the following spring for a repeat performance. Lysimachia and ivy are worth keeping (the lysimachia will virtually die back in winter, but grows again next spring). The mimulus can be composted and more grown from seed or bought in for the following year.

YOU WILL NEED

Plants
6 *Mimulus* × *hybridus* (monkey musk)
1 *Begonia* F1 'Illumination Orange'
(trailing tuberous begonia)
1 *Euonymus fortunei* 'Emerald 'n' Gold'
2 *Lysimachia nummularia* 'Aurea'
(golden creeping Jenny)
1 *Hedera helix* cv. (cream-variegated ivy)

Container
Plastic coated wire hanging basket measuring
35cm (14in) diameter

Position
Shade or semi-shade

Begonia F1
'Illumination Orange'
(trailing tuberous begonia)

Euonymus fortunei
'Emerald 'n' Gold'

Hedera helix cv. (cream-
variegated ivy)

Mimulus ×hybridus
(monkey musk)

Lysimachia
nummularia 'Aurea'
(golden creeping Jenny)

Salvia farinacea 'Victoria'

Plectranthus coleoïdes 'Marginatus'

Lysimachia 'Golden Falls'

Tagetes cvs. (orange and lemon French marigolds)

Marigold Pot

◆

Blue and golden yellow is a marvellous colour combination for bedding schemes and plants in pots. Rather than masses of blooms crowded together, this arrangement uses the two colours in groups, with spaces of foliage between them. In many cases less is more, and I think that gaps of foliage help relax the eye and enable individual flowers and colours to be better appreciated. Plant up in late spring.

Assuming that this arrangement will be seen from the front, the first task is to position the five *Salvia farinacea* 'Victoria' together in a group, about 8cm (3in) apart, towards the middle-back. This elegant salvia can be bought as small plants or raised from seed. The newer variety *S. f.* 'Striata' is possibly even lovelier, bearing silvery stems and calyces from which the blue flowers emerge. They rise to some 45cm (18in) and will add height.

To each side of the container and at the very back, position three *Plectranthus coleoïdes* 'Marginatus'. This aromatic plant, with variegated, slightly fleshy leaves, is more often grown as a houseplant, but makes admirable cover for the sides of a summer container. The trailing stems are quite brittle in comparison with those of ivy. It is a quick-growing plant which roots easily from cuttings.

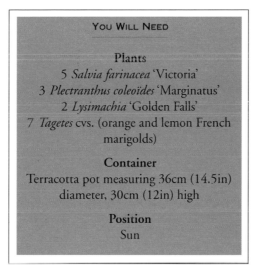

YOU WILL NEED

Plants
5 *Salvia farinacea* 'Victoria'
3 *Plectranthus coleoïdes* 'Marginatus'
2 *Lysimachia* 'Golden Falls'
7 *Tagetes* cvs. (orange and lemon French marigolds)

Container
Terracotta pot measuring 36cm (14.5in) diameter, 30cm (12in) high

Position
Sun

Find a couple of slots along the front for two more trailing plants, of *Lysimachia* 'Golden Falls'. This rather luscious plant bears bright green leaves and generous clusters of rich gold flowers which appear with regularity and reliability all summer.

Having arranged these tall and trailing plants, fill any gaps with compact orange and lemon French marigolds, mixing them well so that they pop out of the foliage here and there. When all are in place, carefully fill in around the roots with compost.

Attacks from slugs, which seem to have a preference for the lemon varieties, killed some off while we were away for a week. Steps need to be taken to protect these plants from slugs and snails. The remaining few marigolds, however, clumped up nicely and made a bold golden splash to the front of the pot.

At the end of the season lift and repot the plectranthus which can overwinter as a houseplant. It needs good light and a constantly warm temperature – minimum 13°C (55°F) – to thrive. Take cuttings for next year. *Lysimachia* 'Golden Falls' can be kept over winter in a cool, bright, frost-free place, but the other plants can all be composted.

Shallow Bowl for a Shady Position

◆

Sometimes a large container can be planted to give the impression of a border. This elevates container gardening above mere assemblages of bedding plants and proves that you can express your tastes in gardening even on a balcony or in a tiny back yard. This bowl for a shady position was planted up in late sping.

The basic idea was to bring together shade-tolerant herbaceous plants for the centre of the container, choosing those which might have been used for dappled shade between trees, or in a border along a north-facing wall between shrubs. The fern is a variety of *Dryopteris affinis* (golden-scaled male fern) bought wrongly labelled as 'Cristata Angusta', which I am sure it is not. *D. affinis* is native to Europe, including the British Isles, and does not die back completely in winter.

Emphasising the all-round effect of this bowl, the fern was planted in the middle, snuggled into place with handsome *Hosta fortunei* var. *Aureomarginata*. Although this is grown mainly for its creamy gold-coloured leaf margins, I also allow it to run up to flower in mid-summer. Many gardeners think that foliage plants like hostas and *Scrophularia auriculata* 'Variegata' should have their flower spikes removed to retain better foliage. I disagree with this. I enjoy the way a plant changes naturally during the seasons and want to watch its progression, even if it ruins the symmetry of my planting. To this combination were added the architectural leaves of *Helleborus orientalis* (Lenten rose).

For the rim of the container take a short-growing *Astilbe* and divide the clump into two. Add to this a potful of *Heuchera* 'Palace Purple' and two of *Ajuga reptans* 'Rainbow' (bugle), arranging them around the edge to look good against the foliage of the centre. Finally fill any gaps between with small plants of pale pink bedding impatiens.

It is fine to leave the plants in the container for the winter, although for the most part they will die back and rest. Compost the impatiens. When the other plants burst back into growth the following spring, the gaps can be plugged by more impatiens and the cycle can continue. Alternatively lift the herbaceous plants and use in the garden if the bowl is to be freed for autumnal plantings.

YOU WILL NEED

Plants
1 *Dryopteris affinis* variety
(golden-scaled male fern)
1 *Hosta fortunei* var. *Aureomarginata*
1 *Helleborus orientalis* (Lenten rose)
1 *Astilbe* cv.
1 *Heuchera* 'Palace Purple'
2 *Ajuga reptans* 'Rainbow' (bugle)
6 *Impatiens* 'Coral' (busy Lizzie)

Container
Wide terracotta bowl measuring
57cm (23in) diameter, 25cm (10in) high

Position
Shade or semi-shade

Dryopteris affinis variety
(golden-scaled male fern)

Hosta fortunei var.
Aureomarginata

Helleborus orientalis
(Lenten rose)

Astilbe cv.

Impatiens 'Coral'
(busy Lizzie)

Heuchera
'Palace Purple'

Ajuga reptans
'Rainbow' (bugle)

Senecio cineraria

Verbena peruviana 'Alba'
(white trailing verbena)

Petunia milliflora
'Fantasy'

Pelargonium cv.
(pink, ivy-leaved
pelargonium)

Tolmiea menziesii
'Taff's Gold'
(piggy back plant)

Petunia Basket

◆

One of the newest bedding plants for containers is the compact, multi-flowering *Petunia milliflora* 'Fantasy' whose dainty blooms are produced in profusion all summer. I tried them out with some more conventional plants in a hanging basket. This was planted up in late spring for a sunny position.

The *milliflora* type of petunias, sometimes sold as 'Junior Petunias', are widely sold at garden centres, but I received my plants by mail order in early spring. They made sturdy plants, ideal for the sides of the basket.

Line the basket and stand on a flowerpot for stability before putting some compost into the base. The rootballs of the young petunias will probably be far too large to push through the gaps in the wire basket from the outside. The solution is to wrap the foliage carefully in a tube of polythene and thread this through from the inside. When all are in place, carefully remove the polythene to release the shoots. Using this method, feed about nine of the twelve petunias into the sides.

I keep a small stock of *Tolmiea menziesii* 'Taff's Gold' (piggy back plant) in the greenhouse. This

YOU WILL NEED

Plants
12 *Petunia milliflora* 'Fantasy'
1 *Tolmiea menziesii* 'Taff's Gold'
(piggy back plant)
3 *Verbena peruviana* 'Alba'
(white trailing verbena)
1 *Senecio cineraria*
2 *Pelargonium* cv. (pink, ivy-leaved pelargonium)

Container
Plastic-coated wire hanging basket measuring 35cm (14in) diameter

Position
Good light

foliage houseplant grows small replicas of itself where the leaf joins its leaf stalk. It is easy to remove a leaf, cut away some of the old leaf blade and push into gritty compost so that the plantlets root. One of these was added into the side of the basket for the mottled gold and green of its leaves. Plant one of the white-flowered trailing verbenas into the sides as well, to give balance to the two that will later be placed in the top.

Having clothed the sides with plants, fill in around their roots and build up the compost levels ready for planting into the top. For the middle *Senecio cineraria* will make an attractive splash of felted, silvery foliage.

Into the spaces around the senecio introduce the remaining three petunias, two verbenas and a couple of dainty, single trailing pelargoniums.

The petunias performed well, flowering right up until the first frosts. Dismantle the planting at the end of the season, potting up the pelargoniums, tolmiea and verbenas to be kept cool, light and frost-free over winter. The petunias can be composted and the senecio either planted out or used for winter containers.

Mediterranean-style Pot

◆

The main drawback when growing plants in containers is the regular watering and feeding they need. To make life easier this composition uses drought-tolerant plants, which should be tough enough to survive short periods of neglect. Use a gritty compost, plant up in late spring and stand in full sun.

From a design point of view this mixture of plants also adds a spiky, Mediterranean touch to the garden and seems particularly suitable for dry gardens, patios and poolsides. Pot up the agave in late spring and stand in a sunny position.

Begin by choosing a statuesque, tree-like plant such as this succulent *Aeonium arboreum* 'Arnold Schwarzkopff', which has rosettes of dark coppery-purple leaves at the end of long, stiff stems. An established *Crassula argentea* (money tree or jade tree) would do equally well. Position this specimen in the middle of the pot. To one side place a large succulent with spiky leaves such as this tender *Agave americana* 'Mediopicta Alba' (century plant), which is to my mind the most attractive of the Mexican century plants. Spiny-edged leaves are smartly marked with green on the outer edge and creamy white inside.

On the other side of the aeonium place a well-established pelargonium. I keep several miniature varieties and chose 'Francis Parrett' for its pink flowers and dark foliage. This will remain small and bushy so that the stem of the aeonium rises above it. Flanking the pelargonium plant two *Sedum sieboldii* 'Mediovariegatum', whose stems of cream-centred, rounded, succulent leaves spring out from the base. To retain the attractive variegation, remove any stems with pale green leaves only.

For trailing effect and for its pale pink flowers and cream-edged leaves which turn reddish pink in the sun, ivy-leaved *Pelargonium* 'L'Elégante' These need plenty of bright sunshine for their warm-coloured flowers to open. A double red flowered portulaca (sun plant) was allowed to spill over the edge. Finally there was just room to slot in a glaucous rosette of *Echeveria glauca*.

At the end of the season all the plants (bar the annual portulaca) are worth potting up and saving in a cool, frost-free greenhouse.

YOU WILL NEED

Plants
1 *Aeonium arboreum* 'Arnold Schwarzkopff'
1 *Agave americana* 'Mediopicta Alba'
(century plant)
1 *Pelargonium* 'Francis Parrett'
(miniature pelargonium)
2 *Sedum sieboldii* 'Mediovariegatum'
1 *Pelargonium* 'L'Elégante'
(trailing ivy-leaved pelargonium)
1 *Portulaca grandiflora* cv. (double red sun plant)
1 *Echeveria glauca*

Container
Terracotta pot measuring 34cm (13in) diameter,
and 26cm (10.5in) high

Position
Sun

Aeonium arboreum
'Arnold Schwarzkopff'

Agave americana
'Mediopicta Alba'
(century plant)

Pelargonium 'Francis
Parrett'
(miniature pelargonium)

Pelargonium 'L'Elégante'
(trailing ivy-leaved
pelargonium)

Sedum sieboldii
'Mediovariegatum'

Echeveria glauca

Portulaca grandiflora cv.
(double red sun plant)

Pelargonium cv. (red zonal pelargonium)

Helichrysum italicum ssp. *microphyllum* (curry plant)

Nolana 'Cambridge

Portulaca grandiflora (double red sun plant)

Aptenia cordifolia 'Variegata'

Drought-tolerant Basket

◆

Many gardeners are put off hanging baskets because of all the watering and feeding they need, which is a pity, because they are so good for brightening and softening dull walls and fences. To help it withstand a dry, windy site this basket is packed full of drought-tolerant plants which can endure a little neglect without withering. Plant up in late spring and hang in a sunny position.

Begin by lining the basket and sitting it on a flowerpot for stability while you plant. A small tray of mixed succulent portulaca will yield enough little plants to fit around the sides. These trailing plants are double-flowered varieties of *Portulaca grandiflora* (sun plant), an annual from Uruguay and Argentina. Their rootballs should be small enough to fit into the mesh from the outside. If they are not, wrap the leaves carefully in a tube of polythene and thread this through from the inside before unwrapping.

Having filled in around the roots with some more compost, place plants in the top of the basket. A bright red, seed-raised, zonal pelargonium was chosen for the middle of the basket. Once it is in place, surround this with three plants of *Helichrysum*

> ### You Will Need
>
> #### Plants
> 6 *Portulaca grandiflora* (double red sun plant)
> 1 *Pelargonium* cv. (red zonal pelargonium)
> 3 *Helichrysum italicum* ssp. *microphyllum* (curry plant)
> 2 *Aptenia cordifolia* 'Variegata'
> 1 *Nolana* 'Cambridge'
>
> #### Container
> Plastic-coated wire hanging basket measuring 30cm (12in) diameter
>
> #### Position
> Sun

italicum ssp. *microphyllum*. This dwarf curry plant starts off as a compact bush of narrow, silvery, curry-scented leaves. As the planting matures its stems rise up to produce heads of yellow flowers. I have never used the leaves in cooking, but apparently they will lend a mild, spicy flavour if chopped and added to salads.

Between the helichrysums add two plants of the South African succulent *Aptenia cordifolia* 'Variegata' for its cream-variegated leaves and small, starry, bright pink flowers. The third plant is *Nolana* 'Cambridge', a member of the potato and tomato family with its origins in the semi-desert regions of Peru and Chile. Tough-looking leaves are joined by rather shy, sky-blue, saucer-shaped flowers which need the sun to open fully. Sadly an overcast spell during photography sent the flowers furling.

Although all these plants can survive short drought periods, they will not thrive unless well cared for. Aim to water them well and apply a liquid feed every week. At the end of the season pot up the aptenia and possibly the nolana to overwinter in bright, cool, frost-free quarters. The curry plant can be planted into the garden.

Spider-plant Trough

◆

Container planting is a potentially expensive undertaking if all the plants have to be bought in at once. For this reason any suitable plants which can be scrounged from house or garden are to be welcomed. The inspiration behind this colourful planting were the *Chlorophytum comosum* 'Vittatum' (spider plants), which though commonly grown as houseplants are not widely used in containers. Plant up in late spring and place in sun or very light shade.

The spider plant is well known for throwing out trailing stems or runners of flowers and young plants. Keen to start an independent life, the plantlets often begin sprouting roots even before they are provided with anything in which to grow.

During the previous summer, detach some of these youngsters and start them off in their own small 9cm (3.5in) pots, moving them on just once so that they fill a 12cm (5in) pot by the time they are used in containers the following summer.

After crocking the trough, place a little compost in the base and position the two spider plants an even distance apart towards the front. Place one *Asteriscus maritimus* 'Gold Coin' at each end of the trough. These small, eastern Mediterranean perennials are relatively new to the container-plant range and bear bright golden-yellow, daisy-like flowers.

Take three bright red trailing ivy-leaved pelargoniums and place one in each back corner and one in the middle. With a little jostling this should adequately fill the trough, but for a background of small, white daisies I dibbled in young, seed-raised plants of white flowered brachycome. Sprinkled through a collection of container plantings, they have a unifying effect. Once they are in position in the trough, fill in around all the roots with potting compost.

This arrangement has the added advantage of being reasonably drought-tolerant. Spider plants have thick, fleshy roots which can store moisture, while pelargoniums and *Asteriscus maritimus* originate from natural habitats where poor, well-drained soil and periods without rain are the norm. The foliage of spider plants which have been growing indoors may be a little fragile and

---

YOU WILL NEED

Plants
2 *Chlorophytum comosum* 'Vittatum'
(spider plant)
2 *Asteriscus maritimus* 'Gold Coin'
3 *Pelargonium* cv. (red trailing ivy-leaved
pelargonium)
5 *Brachycome* 'White Splendour'
(Swan River daisy)

Container
Terracotta trough measuring 60cm (2ft) long,
17cm (7in) wide, 16cm (6.5in) high

Position
Sun or light shade

prone to scorch in full sun, though it will toughen up as the season progresses. The answer to this is to raise them in a cool, frost-free greenhouse – minimum 7°C (45°F). They are also useful in containers destined for shady places.

At the end of the season all the plants except brachycome are worth saving for another year. The ideal method for this is to take short, non-flowering shoots of pelargoniums and asteriscus as cuttings during summer. By autumn they will be well rooted. Both these and stock plants will require light, cool, frost-free conditions to overwinter. Trim older plants back lightly when bringing them in at the end of the season but prune thoroughly in early spring. Spider plants can be potted and brought into the house.

Asteriscus maritimus 'Gold Coin'

Brachycome 'White Splendour' (Swan River daisy)

Chlorophytum comosum 'Vittatum' (spider plant)

Pelargonium cv. (red trailing ivy-leaved pelargonium)

Plumbago auriculata
(Cape leadwort)

Petunia cv. (pink
Grandiflora type)

Nemesia
'Joan Wilder'

Verbena 'Aphrodite'

Petunia
'Surfinia Purple'

Pink and Blue Plumbago Urn

◆

A pot raised on a pedestal like this regal urn offers a fine excuse for some splendid planting. It is amazing how the character of a planted arrangement changes and matures from the first few weeks of the season to the last. When this was first assembled and stood proudly in the garden, there was a neat hoop of *Plumbago auriculata* (Cape leadwort), with the other plants clustering demurely at its feet. This grew and spread into a wonderful Napoleon-hat-shaped mound of pink flowers. Plant up in late spring and stand in a sunny position.

The plumbago can often be found among the conservatory plant selection at a garden centre. However, this showy, blue-flowered, climber can also be grown outside during the summer and was often used in the past to create flamboyant displays of sub-tropical bedding. To tame their wayard stems, young plants are usually trained around a hoop and this was left in place when the plant was placed in the centre of the urn.

The Surfinia petunias are a group of superb, trailing plants which give any container a real presence. These large plants should be used with caution as they can swamp smaller, daintier specimens. Two bright, shocking purple-pink Surfinias were chosen, to position one on each side of the plumbago. With these in place, slot in the three large-flowered, pale pink petunias, three plants of splendid mauve-and-white *Verbena* 'Aphrodite' and one dainty pinkish-blue *Nemesia* 'Joan Wilder' wherever they will fit, in order to knit together for a fine tapestry of different shades.

If a mixture of plants begins to grow in a definite shape, like this Napoleon hat, it can be accentuated by occasionally bending in or cutting out stems.

At the end of the season the plumbago can be carefully extracted and potted up. Originating from South Africa, it needs winter frost protection but can survive low temperatures – minimum 3°C (37°F). To keep plants small, prune back in spring and they will flower in mid to late summer. Verbena and this perennial nemesia can be overwintered as stock plants or, even better, as small plants from cuttings rooted during summer.

While it is theoretically possible to root cuttings of Surfinia petunias and keep mature plants over winter, it is advisable to throw them away and buy new ones each year. They are prone to virus, but new stock should always be virus-free.

YOU WILL NEED

Plants
1 *Plumbago auriculata* (Cape leadwort)
4 *Petunia* 'Surfinia Purple'
4 *Petunia* cv. (pink Grandiflora type)
3 *Verbena* 'Aphrodite'
1 *Nemesia* 'Joan Wilder'

Container
Terracotta pedestal urn measuring
35cm (14in) diameter, 44cm (17.5in) high

Position
Sun

Fuchsia Basket

◆

For an ordinary, unpretentious hanging basket it is hard to beat a combination of fuchsias, trailing pelargoniums and verbena with an underskirt of trailing lobelia. There is no particular theme to this arrangement other than a liking for the plants. Plant up in late spring and hang in a position of sun or very light shade.

As with most summer baskets, planting begins by fitting a liner into place and standing the basket on top of a flowerpot for stability. Place some compost in the base and begin to plant up the sides with trailing *Lobelia* 'Sapphire'. As tiny plants they can easily be fed into the sides from outside.

Fill in with more compost and position *Fuchsia* 'Jack Shahan' in the centre. This particular specimen had been bought as a small plant the previous summer, served its time in a window box

and been overwintered in a frost-free greenhouse. As the central plant for this arrangement, it was to be given a new lease of life. A thorough pruning in spring had payed dividends, as plenty of flowering shoots had been produced. This is a trailing fuchsia with large, elegant flowers.

Into the space around the plant arrange all the remaining plant ingredients, bearing in mind that some of the growth towards the back will not be readily seen. These consist of three double-flowered trailing *Pelargonium* 'Blanche Roche', whose flowers show up brilliantly, especially at dusk. Pink-flowered trailing *Verbena* 'Silver Anne' bears heads of shimmering, pink flowers in great profusion. It pays to be cautious with new plants, so only one specimen of trailing *Petunia* 'Million Bells' was used. I acquired several as young 'plugs' during early spring, to grow on in the greenhouse. At first they sat there making a lot of rather upright, gawky stems and had not begun to trail, even by planting-out time. However, the lone plant in the basket soon proved its worth, bending outwards and opening a profusion of delightful, small, purple flowers with yellow centres.

At the end of the season carefully lift out the fuchsia, pelargoniums and verbenas to be overwintered, frost-free, in a cool, light place. Alternatively take 8cm (3in) cuttings during summer to produce rooted plants for the winter. I am not sure about the perenniality of *Petunia* 'Million Bells', but presume it would be better to buy in more young plants the following year.

You Will Need

Plants
8 *Lobelia* 'Sapphire' (trailing lobelia)
1 *Fuchsia* 'Jack Shahan'
3 *Pelargonium* 'Blanche Roche' (double-flowered trailing geranium)
2 *Verbena* 'Silver Anne' (trailing verbena)
1 *Petunia* 'Million Bells'

Container
Plastic-coated wire hanging basket measuring 35cm (14in) diameter

Position
Sun or light shade

Verbena
'Silver Anne'
(trailing verbena)

Fuchsia 'Jack Shahan'

Pelargonium 'Blanchc
Roche' (double-flowered
trailing geranium)

Petunia 'Million Bells'

Lobelia 'Sapphire'
(trailing lobelia)

Cool Shade Pot

◆

The range of container plants for shady positions in the garden is more restricted than that for full sun, but there are still some exciting choices. All the fuchsias and begonias are suitable candidates, as are impatiens (busy Lizzie) and mimulus (monkey flower). For foliage *Lysimachia nummularia* 'Aurea' (golden creeping Jenny), hedera (ivy), coloured-leaved varieties of *Ajuga reptans* (bugle) and many other herbaceous plants are suitable. Plant up this low pot in late spring and position in light shade.

The inspiration behind this low planting were the splendid New Guinea impatiens teamed with the glazed pot, which has a mottling of blue over very pale brown. The availability of both matt and glazed pots in many colours has made it easier to succeed with container planting. For groups it is sensible to choose different sizes of pots and bowls in matching or blending colours.

New Guinea *impatiens* are now available in a wide range of foliage and flower colours. Marvellously exotic, their flowers, leaves and whole stature are larger than those of conventional busy Lizzies. The story goes that, in New Guinea, selection had already taken place by native gardeners who looked for naturally occurring hybrids and forms. Those with the best flower colour and foliage were planted around their homes. The New Guinea group of impatiens which eventually arrived in the west is still evolving, with ever more stunning variations being grown and marketed. They do need regular dead-

---

YOU WILL NEED

Plants
2 *Impatiens* cv. (New Guinea Type) (busy Lizzie)
1 *Fuchsia* 'Tom West'
1 *Fuchsia* 'Eva Boerg'
3 *Ajuga reptans* 'Rainbow' (bugle)

Container
Glazed terracotta pot measuring 37cm (15in) diameter, 27cm (11in) high

Position
Light shade

---

heading, because the large petals fall and stick to the leaves below, which can disfigure them, especially after rain.

Two impatiens were planted in the centre-back of the pot, their rich pink flowers already open and contrasting with their dark, reddish-coloured foliage. The challenge was to find other plants which would complement them as well as tolerate shade. *Fuchsia* 'Tom West', an old variety dating from 1853, is interesting not just for its flowers, a classic mix of bright pink sepals and purple corolla, but also for leaves irregularly edged with cream and suffused with pink. A hardy upright but lax fuchsia, it will reach 30–60cm (1–2ft). Plant this to one side of the impatiens and select a different type for the other side. Here, *Fuchsia* 'Eva Boerg' was chosen for its white sepals and purple-pink corolla. A bushy but low-growing plant, it is quite tough and hardy in mild areas.

This left a gap at the front. *Ajuga reptans* 'Rainbow' (bugle) seemed just right, as it too has cream-edged, pink-flushed leaves. While sometimes it seems safer to keep coloured-leaved plants separate, on other occasions it pays to experiment as the results can be quite successful.

At the end of the season all the components can be lifted and retained for future use. Pot the impatiens and bring them into a warm, bright place for winter. A conservatory is ideal, or a well-lit position in the house. Fuchsias can be potted and overwintered in a cool, bright, frost-free place. Alternatively, in milder regions, plant them out in the garden, but mound well-rotted compost or soil over their crowns for extra insulation.

The bugle could remain in position as it is an excellent hardy evergreen for autumn, winter and spring container plantings. If it is not required, simply plant into the garden as shade-tolerant ground cover.

Impatiens cv. (New Guinea type)

Fuchsia 'Eva Boerg'

Fuchsia 'Tom West'

Ajuga reptans 'Rainbow' (bugle)

Pelargonium
'Frank Headley
(zonal pelargonium)

Pelargonium cv. (red
zonal pelargonium)

Verbena peruviana 'Alba'
(trailing verbena)

Verbena 'Tenera' (red)
(trailing verbena)

Petunia (pink, dark pink,
cream and blue petunia)

Lobelia erinus cv.
(trailing lobelia)

Bidens ferulifolia

Verbena
'Homestead Purple'
(trailing verbena)

Brachycome 'Tinkerbell'
(Swan River daisy)

Mixed Hanging Basket

◆

This flamboyant mixture of plants in a basket brightened up a north-facing wall all summer. What started off as a relatively demure composition grew wilder and more exuberant as the season wore on. Plant up in late spring and hang in a position of sun or light shade.

For this arrangement a solid plastic basket was chosen, with the hope that it might not dry out so rapidly as a wire type lined with moss or another flexible liner. One step further would be to choose a solid basket fitted with a water reservoir. The main drawback with solid baskets is having to look at the plastic base while plant growth builds up inside. The right plants will quickly achieve a cascade of trailing growth, but for true all-round effect, planting into the sides of a wire basket is hard to beat.

Place some compost in the base and arrange three zonal pelargoniums in the centre. Here two bright red flowered plants were used either side of *Pelargonium* 'Frank Headley'. This pretty variety bears cream-edged, silvery leaves and dainty, salmon-pink flowers. Next take the trailing verbenas, bidens and brachycome. Arrange them evenly around the pelargoniums, favouring the three-quarters of the sides which will be most visible. Just one bidens is responsible for the mass of ferny foliage and yellow flowers shown in the photograph. This native of the southern USA and Mexico may start off as a small, unassuming plant, but rapidly puts out wayward stems. Once the larger plants are in place, use the smaller petunia and trailing lobelia to fill gaps where needed. Then fill in around their roots with compost and water to settle them.

In summer take cuttings of the bidens and verbenas for overwintering. *Verbena* 'Homestead Purple' also makes excellent, floriferous ground cover and has survived −9°C (16°F) in our garden. In late summer take cuttings of the pelargoniums if these are needed. Prune back the bidens if necessary. At the end of the season carefully pot up the verbenas, bidens and pelargoniums. Overwinter in cool, bright, frost-free conditions. Even better, take summer cuttings and keep the young plants.

YOU WILL NEED

Plants
3 *Pelargonium* cv. (red zonal pelargonium)
1 *Pelargonium* 'Frank Headley'
1 *Verbena peruviana* 'Alba' (trailing verbena)
1 *Verbena* 'Homestead Purple' (trailing verbena)
1 *Verbena* 'Tenera' (trailing verbena)
1 *Bidens ferulifolia*
1 *Brachycome* 'Tinkerbell' (Swan River daisy)
4 *Petunia* (pink, dark pink, cream and blue petunia)
3 *Lobelia erinus* cv. (trailing lobelia)

Container
Solid plastic hanging basket measuring 35cm (14in) diameter

Position
Sun or light shade

Aromatic Herb Pot

◆

A pot of culinary herbs should look beautiful, smell delicious and deliver plenty of fresh leaves to use in cooking. No amount of dry herbs can compensate for the intense, permeating flavours of fresh ones. Plant this container in late spring and stand it in a sunny position. Although they will not flourish if left dry for long periods, herbs are generally far more drought-tolerant than the typical bedding plant.

> **YOU WILL NEED**
>
> **Plants**
> 1 *Rosmarinus officinalis* (rosemary)
> 1 *Salvia officinalis* 'Icterina'
> (tricolor sage)
> 1 *Thymus × citriodorus* 'Aureus'
> (golden lemon thyme)
> 1 *Helichrysum italicum* (curry plant)
> 1 *Melissa officinalis* 'Aurea' (lemon balm)
> 1 *Origanum* 'Gold Splash' (marjoram)
>
> **Container**
> Terracotta pot measuring 34cm (13in)
> diameter, 26cm (10.5in) high
>
> **Position**
> Full sun

from, so select this only if you want its distinctive, lemony flavour as opposed to ordinary culinary thyme (*Thymus vulgaris*).

Helichrysum italicum was added for its colour and smell. Its silvery-grey leaves smell distinctly of curry, making it a good talking point. The two herbaceous herbs growing in the back of the container are *Melissa officinalis* 'Aurea' (lemon balm) and *Origanum* 'Gold Splash' (marjoram), both of which die down for the

A successful herb pot should last at least two years and contain a good majority of evergreens, like rosemary, sage and thyme, for winter interest and usefulness. Although rosemary can grow tall in a border, a bushy plant is ideal for the centre of an arrangement. Restricted to a container, in close competition with other herbs and regularly cropped, it should remain within bounds.

To one side of the rosemary place an aromatic sage. For colour *Salvia officinalis* 'Icterina' (tricolor sage), with its sage-green and lime-green leaves, is hard to beat. Take odd leaves for cooking, but also nip out whole shoots if it grows too large. *Thymus × citriodorus* 'Aureus' (golden lemon thyme) is great for cooking too. There are many thymes to choose

winter, but put up plenty of new spring shoots.

The key to success with container-grown herbs is continuous cropping, which keeps them young and fresh. Even so it pays to give all the shrubby herbs a good trimming by about half to two-thirds in spring as they come into growth. This will encourage regeneration of shoots and plenty of fresh, tasty herbs for the following summer.

Keep these herbs growing together for two seasons. Then lift them out in early autumn or spring, and plant in the garden. You could take enough cuttings to start a herb garden. The herbaceous lemon balm and marjoram can be lifted and divided. Replant small portions of roots in groups for large patches of the herbs.

Melissa officinalis 'Aurea'
(lemon balm)

Rosmarinus officinalis
(rosemary)

Origanum 'Gold Splash'
(marjoram)

Helichrysum italicum
(curry plant)

Thymus × citriodorus
'Aureus'
(golden lemon thyme)

Salvia officinalis 'Icterina'
(tricolor sage)

CONTAINERS FOR AUTUMN

AUTUMN IS AN INTERESTING SEASON, represented by colourful leaves, berries and seed heads as well as by the late flowers of chrysanthemums and Michaelmas daisies. It is important that during this busy time, when containers are being planted for autumn, winter and spring interest, the essence of autumn itself is not overlooked.

This becomes even more important when containers form the bulk of a garden, in courtyards and on balconies. Several floors up in a city block of flats a gardener really needs to have a sense of seasons unfolding. In the next few pages are some conventional containers of evergreens and winter-season flowering plants. There are also brassicas (kale), calluna (Scottish heather) and warm, autumnal colours.

Even after flowering, dying stems and seed heads will give the illusion of a naturally fading garden, so avoiding an over-neat appearance. Stylishly planted containers should be able to mimic the combination of shapely outlines and informal contents achievable in well-designed full-scale gardens.

Crimson-and-gold Pot

◆

The colours and textures of foliage can be as important as flowers for autumn containers. Here a splendid purple-and-pink kale dominates a terracotta pot, towering over the branches of *Lonicera nitida* 'Baggesen's Gold'. This useful evergreen shrubby honeysuckle is easy to grow and is often used to lighten up gloomy corners. Tall pots can seem a little bottom-heavy, so a pot of compact *Hebe* 'Early Blue' has been added to cover some of the sides. Plant in autumn and stand in a sunny or lightly shaded position.

Ornamental kales and cabbages are very much part of the autumn container scene. Their full beauty only really lasts until mid-winter, so they should not be viewed as a long-term treat. Despite this, their shapes and colours are unrivalled, making them hard to resist. This container stands raised on bricks in front of our porch behind a bed of plants and the kale was allowed to flower during late spring and early summer.

When the kale was finally pulled up and thrown away, the lonicera took centre stage. What had started as underplanting had doubled its size by the

YOU WILL NEED

Plants
1 *Brassica oleracea* cv. (tall ornamental kale)
1 *Lonicera nitida* 'Baggesen's Gold'
1 *Erica carnea* 'Ann Sparkes' (winter-flowering heather)
1 *Euonymus fortunei* 'Emerald 'n' Gold'
1 *Hebe* 'Early Blue'

Containers
Tall terracotta pot measuring 37cm (15in) diameter, 37cm (15in) high
Small terracotta pot measuring 16cm (6.5in) diameter, 14cm (5.5in) high

Position
Sun or light shade

following autumn and become a waterfall of small, neat, oval leaves. It can stand as a year-round attraction for many years now, lending height to the back of the bed. Its position is west-facing and, though strong afternoon sun does bleach its gold leaves, the effect is attractive.

A gold-leaved, winter-flowering heather, *Erica carnea* 'Ann Sparkes', and golden *Euonymus fortunei* 'Emerald 'n' Gold', originally added to fill gaps at the back of the pot, have been removed to other parts of the garden as they were being quickly swamped. Winter-flowering heathers are useful gap fillers for autumn, winter and spring containers and can can be grown in any soil or potting compost.

Hebe 'Early Blue' is a glaucous, grey-leaved sort similar in general appearance to *H. pinguifolia* 'Pagei' and both seem to be far hardier and more reliable than those with larger, fleshier leaves and long flower spikes. Grown mainly for its foliage, it has pure white spring flowers.

Having enjoyed this arrangement for a year, you could dismantle it and use the plants in the garden, or you could allow it to evolve.

Brassica oleracea cv.
(tall ornamental kale)

Euonymus fortunei
'Emerald 'n' Gold'

Erica carnea 'Ann
Sparkes' (winter-
flowering heather)

Lonicera nitida
'Baggesen's Gold'

Hebe 'Early Blue'

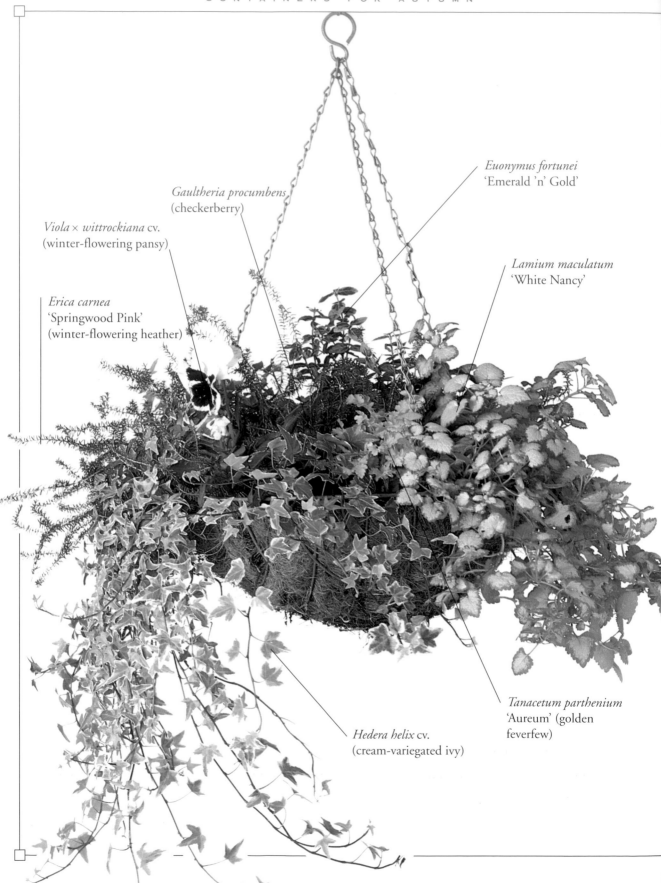

Euonymus fortunei
'Emerald 'n' Gold'

Gaultheria procumbens
(checkerberry)

Lamium maculatum
'White Nancy'

Viola × wittrockiana cv.
(winter-flowering pansy)

Erica carnea
'Springwood Pink'
(winter-flowering heather)

Hedera helix cv.
(cream-variegated ivy)

Tanacetum parthenium
'Aureum' (golden
feverfew)

Recycled Autumnal Basket

◆

When small shrubs and evergreens are used for containers, the same composition can be made to last for several years. This hanging basket was planted one autumn, livened up a house wall throughout winter and spring in a difficult, windy position, then occupied a shady spot under a tree for summer before taking the limelight again. It was photographed during its second autumn, after a thorough tidy-up.

Ideally winter hanging baskets should be kept out of the wind, but this is not always feasible. Even in a wind tunnel between two houses, these plants certainly showed their toughness. The coir liner seemed a good choice to protect their roots and has an advantage over sphagnum moss as birds don't rip tufts from the sides in spring to use for nests. It was decided not to plant up the sides, because of the threat of the wind dry-freezing the plants' roots.

Of the original planting I decided to keep a solid fringe made up of *Erica carnea* 'Springwood Pink' (winter-flowering heather), already showing promising buds. The *Gaultheria procumbens* (checkerberry) was still healthy and there was good, trailing growth provided by variegated ivy and *Lamium maculatum* 'White Nancy' which had flowered beautifully during summer. After unruly growth had been trimmed back and the original ericaceous compost moistened and loosened, there was room for the bright *Euonymus fortunei* 'Emerald 'n' Gold', winter-flowering pansies and a golden tanacetum (feverfew). These new additions will see the arrangement through its second winter.

The growth of the acid-loving gaultheria is relatively slow and this spreading evergreen may need to be rescued from ivy growth periodically. For it to thrive use ericaceous compost and soft water from the rain butt.

In late spring the basket can be dismantled and the euonymus and lamium used as ground cover for dry shade. The checkerberry enjoys shade, but prefers a moist, acid soil. Pot up the ivy for future containers. Alternatively sit the basket on top of a clay pot to make watering easier and keep trailing stems off the ground. The foliage will look cool and soothing in a shady spot.

YOU WILL NEED

Plants

1 *Erica carnea* 'Springwood Pink' (winter-flowering heather)
1 *Gaultheria procumbens* (checkerberry)
1 *Lamium maculatum* 'White Nancy'
1 *Hedera helix* cv. (cream-variegated ivy)
1 *Euonymus fortunei* 'Emerald 'n' Gold'
3 *Viola × wittrockiana* cv. (winter-flowering pansy)
1 *Tanacetum parthenium* 'Aureum' (golden feverfew)

Container

Plastic-coated wire hanging basket measuring 35cm (14in) diameter

Position

Sun or light shade (shade in summer)

Bellis Trough

Houses can look austere unless softened by foliage and flowers, though not all have window ledges wide enough to accommodate planted troughs. A lightweight, plastic window box, however, can easily be balanced on brackets under a window and can be used not just for flamboyant summer flowers, but also for a more subtle display for autumn, winter and spring. This symmetrical arrangement is smart and, in its second year, the ivies will grow into a veil of emerald green across the front. Plant in autumn.

For a long window box use this pair of evergreen *Euonymus japonicus* 'Microphyllus Pulchellus' to give height. It is worth stressing that the plants will hardly grow at all until their first spring, so if you want impact during autumn and winter, choose good-sized plants. *Chamaecyparis pisifera* 'Strathmore' makes a good mound of gold-flecked foliage between the upright shapes.

Having placed the key plants, divide two large pots of plain green ivy into two each and space them out along the front. Any remaining gaps can be filled by red button-flowered bellis and hybrid primroses.

Before filling in around the plants with potting compost, add some bulbs for spring. I used *Tulipa* 'Showwinner',

You Will Need

Plants
2 *Euonymus japonicus* 'Microphyllus Pulchellus'
1 *Chamaecyparis pisifera* 'Strathmore'
(low dwarf conifer)
2 pots (4 plants) of *Hedera helix* cv. (plain green ivy)
4 *Bellis perennis* cv. (double red daisy)
2 *Primula* hybrid (cream-flowered primrose)
6 *Tulipa* 'Showwinner' (Kaufmanniana tulip)
(not illustrated)

Container
Lightweight plastic trough measuring
85cm (34in) long, 14cm (5.5in) wide,
14cm (5.5in) high

Position
Sun or light shade (shade in summer)

a Kaufmanniana type reaching 15cm (6in) high with cheerful red-and-yellow flowers.

In late spring the whole box can be emptied and the three main evergreens planted out either as permanent features or to be used in future containers. Primroses are worth planting in a moist, shaded bed to rest for summer and can be moved into more prominent positions the following autumn. Even bellis can be used again, but are prone to attack by aphids. Potted up, the ivies can develop a full, trailing habit.

Alternatively the box can be kept more or less intact for another year. Move out of full sun for the summer and replace the bellis and primroses with shade-tolerant summer bedding plants such as dainty fuchsias, mimulus or begonias.

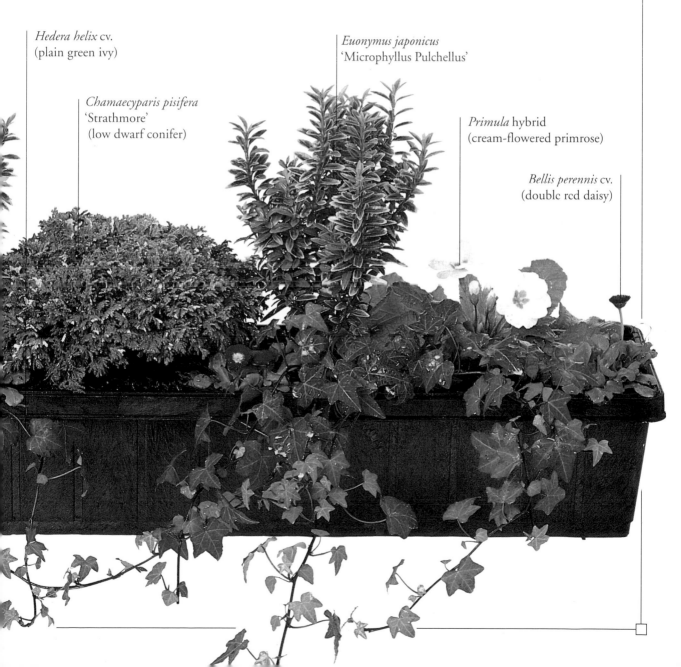

Hedera helix cv.
(plain green ivy)

Chamaecyparis pisifera
'Strathmore'
(low dwarf conifer)

Euonymus japonicus
'Microphyllus Pulchellus'

Primula hybrid
(cream-flowered primrose)

Bellis perennis cv.
(double red daisy)

Viola × *wittrockiana* cv.
(orange winter-flowering
pansy)

Hebe ochracea
'James Stirling'

Euonymus japonicus
'Microphyllus
Pulchellus'

Solanum capsicastrum
(Christmas cherry)

Polystichum setiferum
(soft shield fern)

Thymus vulgaris
(thyme)

Solanum Bowl

◆

A subtle but interesting blend of warm colours, this low bowl could provide the central focus to a collection of three containers placed together. The main season of interest is autumn, but it will go on to decorate winter, spring and perhaps summer too. Plant in autumn and stand in full light for winter, but in semi-shade during summer.

Height is achieved here with dwarf, upright, ever-green *Euonymus japonicus* 'Microphyllus Pulchellus'. This particular plant had already served one winter season in a pot. After spending the following summer planted into a semi-shaded corner of the garden, it transplanted happily into this bowl.

To one side of the euonymus position *Solanum capsicastrum*. The Christmas cherry is becoming a popular choice for autumnal container plantings and tempting displays can be found in the outdoor sections of garden centres. Although hardy in most areas of Britain, this solanum remains attractive only until mid-winter. If its tattiness begins to devalue the rest of the composition, plant it out and replace it with more winter-flowering pansies.

YOU WILL NEED

Plants

1 *Euonymus japonicus* 'Microphyllus Pulchellus'
1 *Solanum capsicastrum* (Christmas cherry)
1 *Polystichum setiferum* (soft shield fern)
1 *Hebe ochracea* 'James Stirling'
1 *Thymus vulgaris* (thyme)
2 *Viola × wittrockiana* cv. (orange winter-flowering pansy)

Container
Painted terracotta bowl measuring 42cm (17in) diameter, 20cm (8in) high

Position
Sun or light shade (light shade in summer)

To the back and side of the euonymus, place a *Polystichum setiferum* (soft shield fern). It pays to cultivate a stock group of these pretty ferns in the garden. Tolerant of most conditions, including dry shade, they produce small replicas of themselves along mature fronds. Either pull off large fernlets and root them into small pots, or lay the whole frond on to conditioned soil or a tray of moist compost. Peg down at intervals and the young ferns will root down and can be separated later.

To the front of the fern arrange *Hebe ochracea* 'James Stirling' for its bronze, scale-like, evergreen foliage. Small, white flowers appear in early summer. To pour over the bowl's front edge, choose thyme, a reliable winter evergreen which doubles as a useful culinary herb. Prune back in spring to maintain fresh foliage. Finally slot in a couple of orange winter-flowering pansies to fill any remaining gaps.

By the end of spring the plants can be carefully separated and used in the garden. Alternatively move the container to a shady spot for the summer, replacing the straggly pansies with mimulus plants.

Pot of Late Flowers and Foliage

◆

This pot of autumnal bloom is aimed at the gardener whose efforts are restricted mainly to containers. On a small patio or strong balcony a series of troughs and boxes can hold not just the seasonal colour provided by transient bedding plants, but a whole range of shrubs, herbaceous perennials, vegetables and herbs too. Plant up this container in spring and stand in a well-lit position so that the plants can grow strongly for a lovely autumnal display.

Although there will be little flower until autumn, there will be plenty of foliage interest. For its solid, rounded shape and fleshy, pale green leaves *Sedum* 'Autumn Joy' (ice plant) can take centre stage. By late summer stems bearing slightly domed heads of light green flower buds will rise up, opening to rich pink flowers in autumn which attract bees. Even in winter the old flower heads look attractive.

Position a Michaelmas daisy behind this. I have used a variety of *Aster amellus* (Italian starwort). It is not quite as easy to grow as the ordinary Michaelmas daisy (*Aster novi-belgii*), but does not suffer from mildew. *A. amellus* loves well-drained soils and its growth comes from twiggy

---

YOU WILL NEED

Plants
1 *Sedum* 'Autumn Joy' (ice plant)
1 *Aster amellus* (Italian starwort)
1 *Salvia officinalis* 'Purpurascens' (purple sage)
1 *Salvia officinalis* 'Icterina' (tricolor sage)
1 *Hedera helix* 'Goldchild' (variegated ivy)
5 *Gladiolus* hybrid (small-flowered white gladiolus)

Container
Painted terracotta pot measuring 40cm (16in) diameter, 30cm (12in) high

Position
Good light

---

stems at the base instead of below ground. At the front of the container fill gaps by arranging one *Salvia officinalis* 'Purpurascens' (purple sage) and one *S. o.* 'Icterina' (tricolor sage). They will add exciting foliage colour as well as providing leaves for use in cooking. Any other gaps can be plugged by the trailing strands of variegated ivy. Before filling in around all the plant roots with potting compost, place a few gladiolus corms at the back of the pot, choosing a dainty, compact type. Put them about 10cm (4in) deep and 5cm (2in) apart. And, even while growing, their sword-shaped leaves will be attractive. Their flowering period is relatively short and the timing somewhat unpredictable, so a good plan if you have a garden or allotment is to plant more there to use for a succession of bloom.

I would leave the container intact during winter, to enjoy the seed heads and continue to use the evergreen sage leaves for cooking. In spring lift and divide the sedum if necessary and regroup plants if desired. Trim the sages to discourage legginess. Alternatively replant all the ingredients into the beds and borders of a garden.

Gladiolus hybrid (small-flowered white gladiolus)

Aster amellus (Italian starwort)

Sedum 'Autumn Joy' (ice plant)

Salvia officinalis 'Icterina' (tricolor sage)

Hedera helix 'Goldchild' (variegated ivy)

Salvia officinalis 'Purpurascens' (purple sage)

Heather Moor in a Trough

◆

On a Scottish heather moor in late summer and autumn *Calluna vulgaris* (heather, or ling) makes a purple carpet interspersed with *Vaccinium vitis-idaea* (native red whortleberry). Plantations of *Pinus sylvestris* (Scots pine) are another feature. By using similar sorts of plant in a pot or trough of ericaceous compost you can create the same effect. Both the calluna and *Gaultheria procumbens* need an acid soil. Plant up in late summer, using ericaceous compost. Choose a position of good light.

Start by positioning the *Pinus mugo* 'Ophir', a golden form of the dwarf Swiss mountain pine. Dwarf forms of Scots pines are available and *Pinus sylvestris* 'Beuvronensis', for instance, could be used instead. Because they are slow-growing, these dwarf pines tend to be expensive to buy and are worth looking after.

One of the many varieties of *Calluna vulgaris* (heather, or ling) can be tucked into place next. Even late-flowering varieties do not continue to bloom much past late autumn, but some have strong foliage colours. *C. v.* 'Sunrise' has golden-yellow leaves in summer which turn orange-red in winter; 'Silver Knight' bears grey foliage and pale mauve flowers which give it a hazy appearance; and 'Winter Chocolate' is a strange one, with yellow-orange summer leaves which darken and become red tipped in winter.

Here, two specimens of *C. v.* 'Dark Star' look stunning with their close, dark green, scale-like foliage and semi-double, pink flowers. Their richness is picked up by the red winter colouring of the *Gaultheria procumbens* (checkerberry).

There is no reason why this small trough should not provide year-round interest until the plants show signs of being cramped. Dwarf pines are such splendid little plants that it seems a shame to jeopardize their health by keeping them in a restricted container for too long. Do not allow the compost to dry out, using soft rainwater in preference to hard tapwater. A slow-release fertilizer suitable for acid-loving plants can be sprinkled over the compost surface in spring. All the plants are used to poor soils in the wild.

Given adequate water, this arrangement could last well for a couple of years, However, I planted the pine out and it has taken well in its new bed of soil. Callunas and gaultheria can be planted out, but only if your garden soil is acid.

YOU WILL NEED

Plants
1 *Pinus mugo* 'Ophir' (golden dwarf mountain pine)
2 *Calluna vulgaris* 'Dark Star' (heather, or ling)
2 *Gaultheria procumbens* (checkerberry)

Container
Terracotta trough measuring 36cm (14.5in) long, 17cm (7in) wide, 17cm (7in) high

Position
Good light (light shade in summer)

Pinus mugo 'Ophir'
(golden dwarf mountain pine)

Calluna vulgaris
'Dark Star'
(heather, or ling)

Gaultheria procumbens
(checkerberry)

Brachyglottis 'Drysdale'

Brassica oleracea cv.
(ornamental kale)

Hedera helix cv.
(cream-variegated ivy)

Silvery Kale Pot

◆

Sometimes the choice of container contributes as much to the success of an arrangement as do the plants themselves. The cold pink and creamy white colours of these kales, combined with silvery foliage, look so much better in this unusually patterned, glazed pot than they would in plain terracotta. In the garden we used this to stand in a border where there was little else to see in autumn. Perched on a couple of bricks so that water could drain freely from the base, the pot rose up gracefully from fading grasses and other small, ground-covering plants. Plant up in early autumn. Full light would be appreciated for this selection.

The first plant to position, in the centre of the pot, is *Brachyglottis* 'Drysdale' (formerly *Senecio* 'Drysdale'). A fine, evergreen foliage shrub, it bears neat, grey-green leaves with wavy margins. Both the leaf undersides and stems are thickly covered with silvery, felt-like hairs.

Beneath this, arrange the three kales, which are widely available during autumn. Once they are set in position, just tilt each rootball slightly so that the 'face' of the kale is directed outwards. There are different varieties and sizes to choose from. For this pot they need to be low, rounded, flat shapes.

You Will Need
Plants
1 *Brachyglottis* 'Drysdale'
3 *Brassica oleracea* cv. (ornamental kale)
3 *Hedera helix* cv. (cream-variegated ivy)
Container
Glazed clay pot measuring 37cm (15in) diameter, 34cm (13in) high
Position
Good light

Although matching colours would be attractive, it seemed a shame not to show off the variations and I could not resist choosing a range of colours. Their crinkly-edged leaves are very attractive. As with all kales they will begin to look a little sad by mid-winter, when growth starts an upward trend which spoils their neat, compact shapes.

There will be gaps between the kales, so push a variegated ivy into each. Choose good-sized ivies, well-furnished with many cascading stems. These will then trail nicely over the edge of the pot. When all the gaps around the roots have been filled with potting compost, the finishing touch consists of carefully pulling out the brachyglottis branches and positioning them between the leaves of the kale so they sit naturally instead of being bunched up.

As the kales will die away by spring, there are two options for the container. The gaps left could be filled with summer-flowering plants such as ivy-leaved pelargoniums or Surfinia petunias. Alternatively the whole lot could be dismantled. *Brachyglottis* 'Drysdale' will make a fine addition to a shrub border. It would be a good idea to prune the long shoots by about half in spring, to keep the bush compact. Pot up the ivies.

Chrysanthemum Pot

◆

This attractive, terracotta pot is graced with an arrangement of plants whose effect can only be described as instant gratification. Imagine a sad planter of slowly withering bedding plants in a prominent position viewed from the house: a quick, early autumn trip to the garden centre for a Yoder chrysanthemum can bring about a rapid transformation. Add an established ivy and a cheap but cheerful *Tanacetum parthenium* 'Aureum' (golden feverfew) and the result is warming and beautiful. Plant in early autumn and stand in good light.

These days we should be referring to chrysanthemums as dendranthemas, but this new name for such familiar plants is, not surprisingly, taking a while to catch on. While in this country we refer to them as 'chrysanths', in America they call them 'mums', and in the trade these American-bred varieties are known as 'Yoder garden mums'. Characteristics include a low dome of growth studded with small flowers, rather like a hardy charm chrysanthemum. For autumn the warm colours are superb and this glowing orange-pink complements the pale terracotta of the pot.

Yoder mums are a good investment, not only because they deliver a long-lasting display. In most

> **YOU WILL NEED**
>
> **Plants**
> 1 *Dendranthema* cv. Yoder type
> (chrysanthemum)
> 1 *Hedera helix* cv. (cream-variegated ivy)
> 1 *Tanacetum parthenium* 'Aureum'
> (golden feverfew)
>
> **Container**
> Terracotta pot measuring
> 30cm (12in) diameter, 30cm (12in) high
>
> **Position**
> Good light

areas they are hardy and can be kept from year to year. When the autumnal show has finished, move the plant into garden soil and let it establish. In spring, just as new growth is starting, prune it back quite hard, by at least two-thirds. Then, for a repeat of that dome-like mound of flowers, pinch out the tips of the resulting shoots to encourage a branching shape. Buds will form on the ends of the shoots, so you will also be able to enjoy a fine display the following autumn.

Personally I find the dumpy shape of these plants difficult to assimilate into the kind of informal borders I enjoy in my garden. I tend to pinch them back less and enjoy a more natural, informal habit. They are, though, ideal for containers and for those who like to create formal patterns with their plants. Really keen Yoder mum growers can buy collections of young plants in spring and grow them on, which is harder work, but means more plants for less money.

To my mind, the sight and smell of chrysanthemums is very reminiscent of autumn and they belong in that season. Although potted indoor chrysanthemums are available all year round, I would not be without the hardy outdoor types.

Dendranthema cv. Yoder type (chrysanthemum)

Tanacetum parthenium 'Aureum' (golden feverfew)

Hedera helix cv. (cream-variegated ivy)

Asplenium scolopendrium
(hart's tongue fern)

Viola tricolor
(heartsease pansy)

Blechnum penna-marina

Cyclamen hederifolium

Hedera helix cv.
(cream-variegated ivy)

Fern and Cyclamen Pot

◆

Containers for the autumn, winter and spring often rely heavily on evergreens, which tend towards a formal effect that may not suit all tastes. Schemes for pots and troughs can be devised using less formal plantings, but it helps to have a clear view of what the finished product is supposed to look like in order to avoid a hotch-potch. In this pot the contents are designed to resemble the rather wild style of planting you might find in a woodland garden, sprouting up under trees in the process of losing their leaves. Plant in early autumn and stand in light shade.

Large gardens can be planted with a tidy, formal area by the house gradually dissolving to wild wooded areas towards the end. In addition to their smart planted pots, container gardeners can introduce an enjoyable knitting together of woodland plants without the accompanying wood.

The main specimen here, which should be positioned first, is the evergreen *Asplenium scolopendrium* (hart's tongue fern). Easy to grow, it thrives in most soils and likes dappled shade.

The next plant to take it place in front of this, should be the pretty, autumn-flowering *Cyclamen*

YOU WILL NEED

Plants
1 *Asplenium scolopendrium*
(hart's tongue fern)
1 *Cyclamen hederifolium*
2 *Blechnum penna-marina*
2 *Hedera helix* cv. (cream-variegated ivy)
4 *Viola tricolor* (heartsease pansy)

Container
Painted green terracotta pot measuring
25cm (10in) diameter, 23cm (9in) high

Position
Light shade (shade in summer)

---

hederifolium. The pink blooms of this southern European native are jewel-like and the little plant is fascinating. After flowering, green seed pods are pulled back to the ground on coiled stalks. Ants, attracted by a sticky, jelly-like substance surrounding the ripe seeds, will disperse the seeds a little way from the parent and these eventually germinate if the soil is not over-disturbed, forming a colony. I advocate buying plants in bud as these are easier to establish than dry corms. The leaves, which tend to emerge after the flowers, are beautifully patterned.

The next plants to install are a couple of clumps or potfuls of another evergreen fern, *Blechnum penna-marina.* A relative of the native hard fern, this comes from Australia and South America. Although this spreading fern dislikes alkaline soils, it seems to survive in neutral as well as acid types.

All that remains, then, is to fill any remaining gaps around the edges with ivy and *Viola tricolor* (heartsease pansy). As always, spend time arranging the leaves of one plant through another so that they seem to have been growing together for some while. These plants can be maintained together permanently or moved to the garden in spring.

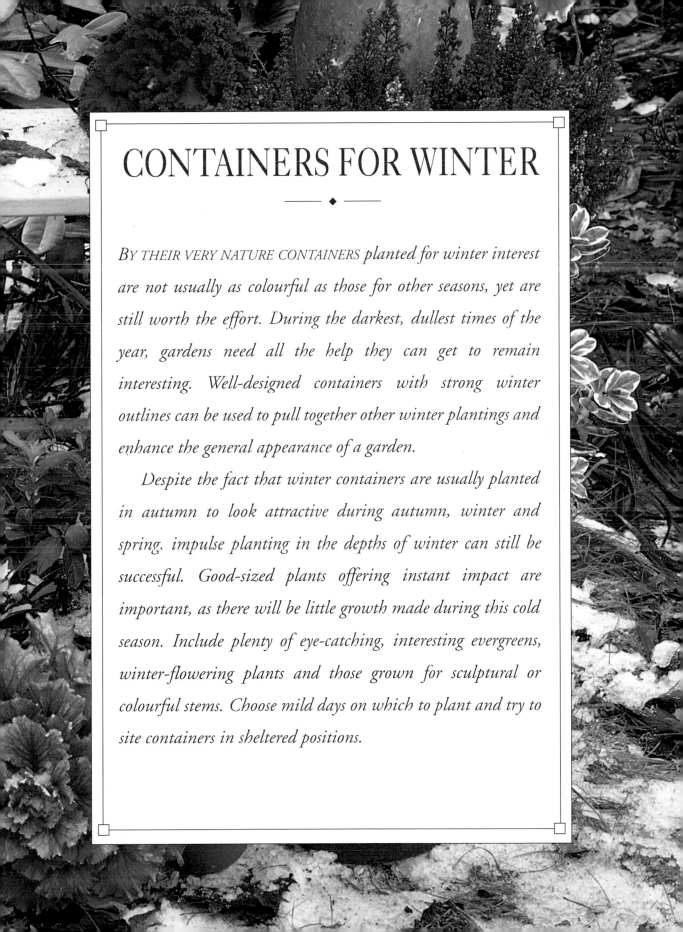

CONTAINERS FOR WINTER

—— ◆ ——

BY THEIR VERY NATURE CONTAINERS *planted for winter interest are not usually as colourful as those for other seasons, yet are still worth the effort. During the darkest, dullest times of the year, gardens need all the help they can get to remain interesting. Well-designed containers with strong winter outlines can be used to pull together other winter plantings and enhance the general appearance of a garden.*

Despite the fact that winter containers are usually planted in autumn to look attractive during autumn, winter and spring, impulse planting in the depths of winter can still be successful. Good-sized plants offering instant impact are important, as there will be little growth made during this cold season. Include plenty of eye-catching, interesting evergreens, winter-flowering plants and those grown for sculptural or colourful stems. Choose mild days on which to plant and try to site containers in sheltered positions.

A Pot of Gold

◆

Unusual and colourful evergreens make this arrangement in a cheerful, terracotta pot successful. Plant in autumn, stand the container in a bright position for winter, then move into semi-shade for summer.

The tallest of the plants, *Osmanthus heterophyllus* 'Goshiki', is a handsome, slow-growing, evergreen shrub easily confused with holly. The leaves bear strong prickles along the margins and in this variety are green, marked with splashes of golden yellow. Although I usually avoid placing two, never mind four different variegated or coloured-leaved plants together for fear of dreadful clashes, I broke my own rule here. I rather like the effect of the mottled osmanthus leaves in the background, with gold-variegated ivy and thyme in the foreground divided by the starburst made by leaves of striking *Carex morrowii* 'Fisher's Form'.

Possibly the reason these bright, gilded plants blend so well together is the backdrop of dark, rounded, deep maroon leaves provided by *Bergenia* 'Wintermärchen' (elephant's ears). All that was needed to add a final touch of richness to the planting was one bright red hybrid primrose. This

---

YOU WILL NEED

Plants
1 *Osmanthus heterophyllus* 'Goshiki'
1 *Bergenia* 'Wintermärchen'
(elephant's ears)
1 *Carex morrowii* 'Fisher's Form'
3 *Thymus* × *citriodorus* 'Aureus'
(golden lemon thyme)
2 *Hedera helix* cv. (gold-variegated ivy)
1 *Primula* hybrid (red primrose)

Container
Terracotta pot measuring
35cm (14in) diameter, 27cm (11in) high

Position
Good light (light shade in summer)

---

is liable to stop flowering during colder winter periods, but can be kept going if the whole container is stood inside the shelter of a brightly lit, well-ventilated, unheated porch.

Position the osmanthus towards the back, as this container is planned to be viewed mainly from one direction. Slot the bergenia behind to fill the gap and settle the carex into place just to the front of the osmanthus but slightly off centre. Place the three thymes in position evenly around the areas of side visible from the front and put the ivies between them. Create a gap for the primrose to one side before making final adjustments, so that all the plants are at the correct heights and favourable angles. Fill in around the roots with compost.

A handful of slow-release fertilizer in spring will be sufficient to keep the plants growing strongly. Replace the primrose when necessary and trim scruffy ivy stems back in autumn before again placing the container in a prominent position. Eventually the main plants can be used to great effect in borders.

Osmanthus heterophyllus 'Goshiki'

Bergenia 'Wintermärchen' (elephant's ears)

Carex morrowii 'Fisher's Form'

Thymus × citriodorus 'Aureus' (golden lemon thyme)

Primula hybrid (red primrose)

Hedera helix cv. (gold-variegated ivy)

Green-and-gold Long Trough

◆

This lightweight, plastic trough is identical to that on pages 96–7. They make up a pair which are permanently slung on brackets beneath the windows at the back of our house. Window boxes can transform the walls of ordinary houses and, together with climbers, are excellent for drawing the eye away from ugly drainpipes. Plant up in autumn and use in a position of good light or light shade.

The feature plants here are evenly spaced *Chamaecyparis lawsoniana* 'Ellwood's Gold' . For a formal effect in autumn, winter and spring, this slow-growing conifer is hard to beat, having a compact shape and gold-coloured young growth which gives it a fresh, light appearance. Should this conifer be planted out into the garden, it will reach only about 1.8m (6ft) in 20 years.

Having spaced the conifers out first, position a good-sized winter-flowering heather in between them. These are such good value, as they are often showing buds in autumn, which open to give a long-lasting display of flowers. The many hybrids of both *Erica carnea* and *Erica* × *darleyensis* can withstand chalk and will grow happily on most well-drained soils. Here *E. carnea* 'R. B. Cooke' is in tight bud, but clear pink flowers will open as winter advances.

The other key plants which give this box its character are the mop-headed *Carex hachijoensis* 'Evergold' (sedge) whose tousled leaves have been allowed to flop over each end. This is yet another example of an evergreen plant which seems happy

YOU WILL NEED

Plants
2 *Chamaecyparis lawsoniana* 'Ellwood's Gold'
(dwarf conifer)
1 *Erica carnea* 'R. B. Cooke'
(winter-flowering heather)
2 *Carex hachijoensis* 'Evergold' (sedge)
4 *Hedera helix* cv. (variegated ivy)
2 *Primula* hybrid (cream primrose)
3 *Ajuga reptans* 'Burgundy Glow' (bugle)

Container
Plastic window box measuring 85cm (34in) long,
14cm (5.5in) wide, 14cm (5.5in) high

Position
Good light or light shade
(light shade in summer)

to be planted into soil in spring, but lifted back out for autumn container plantings.

All that remains is to provide a screen of ivy over the front of the trough and plug the gaps left between the main plants. Cream-coloured hybrid primroses have been used here, though winter-flowering pansies or bellis would be a good alterative.

Any remaining gaps are being colonized by *Ajuga reptans* 'Burgundy Glow' (bugle). This small, evergreen, ground-covering plant is excellent for autumn plantings. Its foliage is of year-round interest and is joined by short spikes of blue flowers in late spring. One larger pot is often better value than several smaller ones from the garden centre. Remove the plant from its pot and

identify different rosettes of growth at the top. Cut through the running stems which connect one rosette to another and it becomes easy to split the clump into several pieces.

Bulbs of dwarf narcissus could be added to push up through the other plants in spring.

There is no reason why the plants in this box should not be allowed to grow together for several years. The ideal course of action would be to remove the whole box to summer quarters in light shade and replace it with an identical box full of summer colour. Alternatively, in late spring, all the components could be planted out in the garden (the ivies should go into pots if they are to be used in a container again).

Ajuga reptans 'Burgundy Glow' (bugle)

Hedera helix cv. (variegated ivy)

Erica carnea 'R. B. Cooke' (winter flowering heather)

Chamaecyparis lawsoniana 'Ellwood's Gold' (dwarf conifer)

Carex hachijoensis 'Evergold' (sedge)

Primula hybrid (cream primrose)

Leucothoë walteri
'Rainbow'

Viola × *wittrockiana* cv.
(red winter-flowering
pansy)

Hedera helix 'Koniger'
(needlepoint ivy)

Saxifraga 'Aureopunctata'

Primula hybrid
(primrose)

Hedera helix cv.
(variegated ivy)

Leucothoë and Primrose Basket

◆

For a reliable winter hanging basket the first task is to search for a bold, solid evergreen to lend a dome-like shape to the middle of the arrangement. Then, to avoid staring at bare sides all winter, you either have to mask them with long strands of dangling ivy or plant into the sides themselves. Assemble the basket in autumn to last through until spring, or plant up in good light during winter for a quick burst of instant colour.

My first choice of a dome-like evergreen would probably be *Euonymus fortunei* 'Emerald 'n' Gold' or *E. f.* 'Silver Queen', but deciding to ring the changes I opted for *Leucothoë walteri* 'Rainbow' in this arrangement. As it is a lime-hating plant, use ericaceous compost for good results. This does not seem to affect the performance of the other plants.

Having mossed or otherwise lined the sides of a plastic-coated wire basket, place a little compost in the base and begin pushing small plants through the holes. This is a time-consuming process as the primroses have quite large rootballs. Each one will have to be removed from its pot, the top wrapped

---

YOU WILL NEED

Plants
7 *Primula* hybrid
(primrose, mixed colours)
2 *Saxifraga* 'Aureopunctata'
1 *Hedera helix* cv. (variegated ivy)
3 *Hedera helix* 'Königer'
(needlepoint ivy)
1 *Leucothoë walteri* 'Rainbow'
2 *Viola × wittrockiana* cv.
(red winter-flowering pansy)

Container
Plastic-coated wire hanging basket
measuring 35cm (14in) diameter

Position
Sun or light shade; sheltered

---

carefully in a tube of polythene and the plant pushed through the hole from the inside out. Push compost under the rootball to support it and unwrap the plant so that its leaves splay over the basket on the outside. Use up most of the hybrid primroses around the sides of the basket facing front, then fill in gaps with *Saxifraga* 'Aureo-punctata' and ivies, which tend to have smaller root systems which can be pushed through.

When the sides are well furnished, put more compost in the base if necessary to raise the leucothoë to the correct height. Put a few ivies, primroses and winter-flowering pansies in remaining gaps around the top before finally filling in with compost.

In spring bring the basket down and dismantle it. Use the leucothoë in the garden if your soil is acid, or in a pot of ericaceous compost if it is not. The gold-splashed saxifraga can be used in a rock garden or dry garden and the primroses can be planted in a shaded position to rest in the garden until required again for autumn plantings. Discard the pansies and pot up the ivies.

A White Winter Trough

◆

Colour theming can be as much fun in containers as it is in garden beds and borders. Focusing on one or two colours makes plant selection easier when faced with such bewildering choice. This trough is brightened up with white-flowered plants, which show up well against the greenery of plain and variegated foliage. Against the back drop of a red brick wall even the tiny flowers of the *Sarcococca confusa* (Christmas box) are notice-able. Plant this container during mild winter periods at any time after the *Arum italicum* ssp. *italicum* 'Marmoratum' has come into growth. A sunny position or semi-shade will be best for winter.

YOU WILL NEED

Plants
1 *Sarcococca confusa* (Christmas box)
1 *Arum italicum* ssp. *italicum* 'Marmoratum'
1 *Helleborus niger* 'Potter's Wheel'
(Christmas rose)
1 *Euonymus fortunei* 'Silver Queen'
2 *Hedera helix* cv. (cream-variegated ivy)
1 *Pulmonaria officinalis* 'Sissinghurst White'
(lungwort)
2 *Ajuga reptans* 'Braunherz' (bugle)
6 *Galanthus elwesii* (snowdrop)

Container
Terracotta trough measuring 60cm (2ft) long,
17cm (7in) wide, 16cm (6.5in) high

Position
Sun or light shade

The two tallest plants should be positioned in the trough first. The Christmas box is a rather plain evergreen often used as shade-tolerant ground cover. It also copes well in dry soil when established. What lifts it out of the ordinary is the perfume released from its small, white blooms. Group this plant with a good clump of the arum and place them in the centre of the trough towards the back.

To one side of these place a beautiful *Helleborus niger* 'Potter's Wheel' (Christmas rose), considered to be the finest form of the species. To be sure of a Christmas rose actually producing its flowers, it pays to choose one in bud. If none is available at planting time in autumn, it might be worth substituting it with a few white, winter-flowering pansies. When a hellebore becomes available, or one develops a flower in the garden, simply transfer the pansies to the garden and lift the hellebore to plant in the trough. This is exactly what I did and it bloomed for quite a long period.

To balance the hellebore place a *Euonymus fortunei* 'Silver Queen' to the other side. In the garden this worthy evergreen with neat, cream-edged leaves will grow quite tall – to about 2.1m (7ft) – and can be wall-trained. To keep it neat for a container simply prune out long shoots to maintain a dumpy shape.

All that remains is to place a good-sized cream-variegated ivy at each end of the trough and plug other gaps with white-flowered *Pulmonaria officinalis* 'Sissinghurst White' and dark-leaved *Ajuga reptans* 'Braunherz'. When they are for sale, buy a couple of pots of *Galanthus elwesii* and plant this large flowered snowdrop here and there along the front of the trough. Alternatively lift small clusters of bulbs from established groups in the garden.

This container could be maintained for several years by adding a slow-release fertilizer in spring. Place in semi-shade for the summer. Alternatively, dismantle and plant the contents in the garden.

Arum italicum ssp. *italicum* 'Marmoratum'

Sarcococca confusa (Christmas box)

Euonymus fortunei 'Silver Queen'

Ajuga reptans 'Braunherz' (bugle)

Helleborus niger 'Potter's Wheel' (Christmas rose)

Galanthus elwesii (snowdrop)

Hedera helix cv. (cream-variegated ivy)

Pulmonaria officinalis 'Sissinghurst White' (lungwort)

Silver and Black

◆

There is so much that is green and gold about winter evergreens that a combination of silvery *Santolina chamaecyparissus* (cotton lavender) and black *Ophiopogon planiscapus* 'Nigrescens' is refreshingly different. *Primula* 'Blue Riband' reinforces the metallic effect. Plant this hanging basket in autumn, to be enjoyed until late spring the following year. A position of good light will be beneficial.

The cotton lavender is often seen in plantings where its ability to withstand summer heat and dry, impoverished soil comes into play. However, it also makes a useful winter container plant. Its neat, dumpy shape can be maintained from year to year by a good shearing over in spring to remove a lot of the previous year's growth.

Stand the basket on a flowerpot in the usual way. Line with moss or other liner, place some compost in the base and begin to plant up the sides. Bear in mind that only the front-facing two-thirds of the sides need the best plants, as the back is usually hidden against the wall or fence. Take three plants of primula and carefully wrap each one in a tube of polythene. You can then thread them through the sides of the basket from inside to

---

YOU WILL NEED

Plants
6 *Primula* 'Blue Riband'
5 *Hedera helix* cv. (cream-variegated ivy)
1 *Santolina chamaecyparissus*
(cotton lavender)
3 *Ophiopogon planiscapus* 'Nigrescens'
6 *Iris* 'Joyce'

Container
Plastic-coated wire hanging basket
measuring 35cm (14in) diameter

Position
Sun

---

out. Fill up gaps with sprigs of rooted ivy, but save three large plants for the top.

Position the cotton lavender in the top, with three ophiopogons around it. These hardy evergreens, which resemble small, black spider plants, reproduce themselves by sending up smaller plants around them to form small colonies. Any remaining gaps in the top of the basket can be filled with ivy and primulas. Before filling in with compost, arrange all the plants so that there are as few gaps as possible. Take six bulbs of *Iris* 'Joyce', a *reticulata* type, and place them between the plants in the top. These will rise up to open their exquisite, blue flowers on short stalks in early spring.

By late spring it will be time to dismantle this hanging basket. Plant the cotton lavender in a sunny position in the garden, where the soil is well drained. A similar site would suit the ophiopogon, which will grow in sun or shade. The primulas can be rested either in pots or, ideally, in the ground in a moist, shady place (protect against slugs) and the ivies can be potted up. Find the iris bulbs and plant them 5cm (2in) deep where they are to flower next spring.

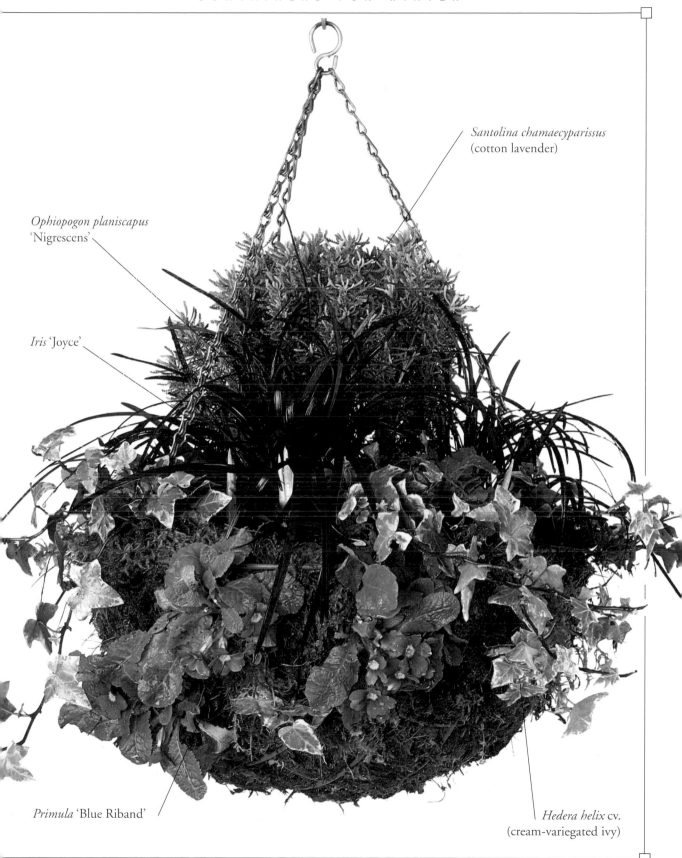

Santolina chamaecyparissus
(cotton lavender)

Ophiopogon planiscapus
'Nigrescens'

Iris 'Joyce'

Primula 'Blue Riband'

Hedera helix cv.
(cream-variegated ivy)

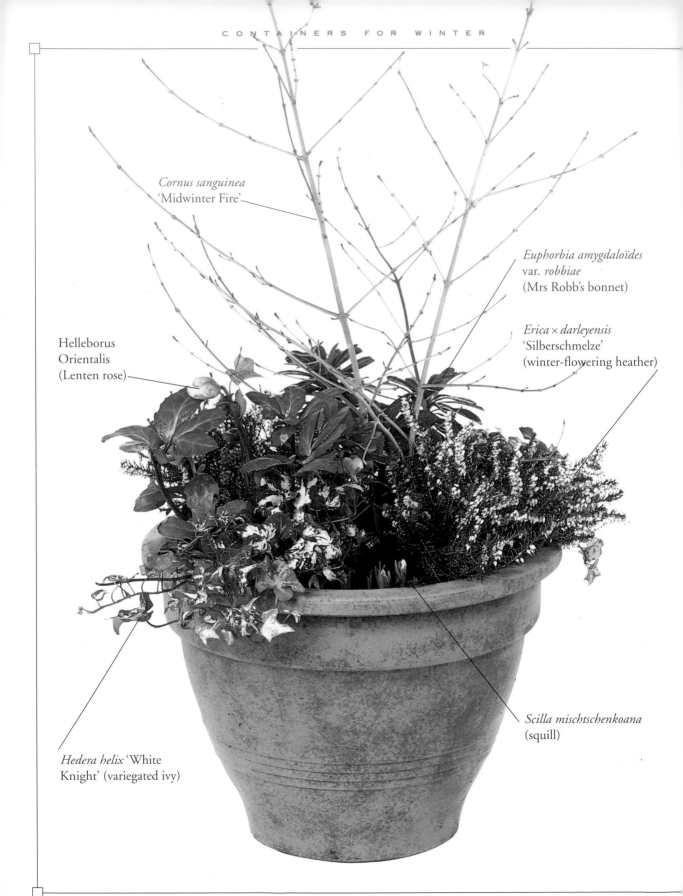

Cornus sanguinea
'Midwinter Fire'

Euphorbia amygdaloïdes
var. *robbiae*
(Mrs Robb's bonnet)

Erica × darleyensis
'Silberschmelze'
(winter-flowering heather)

Helleborus
Orientalis
(Lenten rose)

Scilla mischtschenkoana
(squill)

Hedera helix 'White
Knight' (variegated ivy)

Stems and Foliage

◆

Some of the most colourful winter stems belong to the dogwoods. *Cornus alba* 'Sibirica' has brilliant red stems, while those of *C. sanguinea* 'Midwinter Fire' are a glorious, warm orange with overtones of shrimp pink. It is a young plant of the latter which, carefully dug up from the garden, forms the main feature of this pot, though these plants can easily be bought in pots from the garden centre instead. Plant this container in autumn, to be enjoyed throughout the winter and spring. Place in a sunny spot to illuminate the stems.

The secret of growing dogwoods (and willows) for their colourful stems is to cut them back hard every spring, just as their buds are about to burst. This, known as 'stooling', involves cutting every stem down to within a bud or two of the older wood from which it has grown, so that a system of older stems builds up close to the ground with the newer, more colourful ones rising straight upwards. The prunings can be used as cuttings, which will root in water. Hardwood cuttings can be taken at any time during winter. This way a group can be formed in the garden, from which the odd plant can be borrowed for a container.

Having positioned the dogwood, completion is simply a matter of arranging the other plants around it. *Euphorbia amygdaloïdes* var. *robbiae* (Mrs Robb's bonnet) can be slotted in behind. This spreading, ground-cover plant is a great evergreen gap filler and makes heads of lime-green flowers in spring, when it reaches heights of 45–60cm (18in–2ft). *Erica × darleyensis* 'Silberschmelze' (winter-flowering heather) is useful as it can tolerate even alkaline soils. This reliable, long-flowering plant will be smothered with white blooms throughout winter.

A good clump of red-stemmed *Hedera helix* 'White Knight' (variegated ivy) and some spring-flowering bulbs will complete the arrangement. I used *Scilla mischtschenkoana* (squill), which opens its first pale blue flowers close to the soil in late winter, lasting for several weeks.

To inject some summer interest, plant *Clematis × durandii* for its blue flowers. Prune this back in late autumn. Alternatively, dismantle it and plant out in the garden.

YOU WILL NEED

Plants
1 *Cornus sanguinea* 'Midwinter Fire'
3 *Euphorbia amygdaloïdes* var. *robbiae*
(Mrs. Robb's bonnet)
1 *Helleborus orientalis* (Lenten rose)
2 *Erica × darleyensis* 'Silberschmelze'
(winter-flowering heather)
2 *Hedera helix* 'White Knight' (variegated ivy)
5 *Scilla mischtschenkoana* (squill)

Container
Painted terracotta pot measuring
40cm (16in) diameter, 27cm (11in) high

Position
Good light (sun or light shade in summer)

Corkscrew Hazel Pot

◆

Plants with attractive stems make lovely winter features combined with favourite evergreens. Some, like the *Corylus avellana* 'Contorta' in this glazed clay pot, are sculptural. Plant this combination in autumn, or during a mild spell in winter. Stand in good light for winter, but move to a position of semi-shade for summer.

The key plants to position are the hazel and shapely *Drimys lanceolata* (mountain pepper). This sweetly aromatic, evergreen shrub, whose leaves have a spicy smell when crushed, is becoming more widespread in cultivation. It hails originally from south-eastern Australia and Tasmania, which has raised concerns regarding its hardiness, though it has laughed at cold winters in my garden. The dark green leaves are paler beneath and younger stems are a striking purple-red. The small, spring, creamy-white flowers are not massively showy, but contrast well with the rest of the shrub.

To fill the gap to one side, position a bergenia. These worthy evergreens make a reliable winter display and are useful for the solid shapes their leaves provide. On the other side arrange a good clump of

---

YOU WILL NEED

Plants
1 *Corylus avellana* 'Contorta'
(twisted hazelnut)
1 *Drimys lanceolata* (mountain pepper)
1 *Bergenia cordifolia* 'Redstart'
(elephant's ears)
1 *Arum italicum* ssp. *italicum*
'Marmoratum'
1 *Hedera helix* cv. (plain green ivy)
2 *Lamium maculatum* 'White Nancy'
(dead nettle)

Container
Glazed clay pot measuring
36cm (14.5in) diameter, 30cm (12in) high

Position
Sun or light shade
(light shade for summer)

Arum italicum ssp. *italicum* 'Marmoratum'. This is a wonderful perennial grown for its marbled, arrow-shaped leaves which appear in autumn and grow through-out winter and spring, disappearing at the same time as its spathe-and-spadix flowers become evident. These are followed by short sticks of bright orange-red, poisonous berries which need to be removed if children are about. It is worth establishing a colony of these plants in the garden as useful ground cover and to be raided for other containers.

Finishing off the container is then a matter of filling in the gaps at the front with ivy and *Lamium maculatum* 'White Nancy' or a similar 'dead' nettle grown for its attractive foliage.

This planted pot really needs to be left undisturbed for a few years so that the plants can thicken up and grow into each other. It will only ever be a subdued display. A dose of slow-release fertilizer in spring will be enough to see them through the summer. If planting out, remember that the hazel can reach a height of 4.5m (15ft) and *Drimys lanceolata* will reach 1.8–2.1m (6–7ft).